THE DEVIL KNOWS LATIN

THE DEVIL KNOWS LATIN

Why America Needs the Classical Tradition

E. CHRISTIAN KOPFF

University of Colorado–Boulder

ISI BOOKS

Intercollegiate Studies Institute
Wilmington, Delaware
1999

Cataloging-in-Publication Data

Kopff, E. Christian.
    The Devil knows Latin : why America needs the classical tradition / by E. Christian Kopff. ~1st ed. ~Wilmington, DE : Intercollegiate Studies Institute, 1998.

    p. cm.

    includes index

    ISBN 1-882926-25-0
    1. Civilization, Classical~Study and teaching (Higher) ~United States. 2. Classical education~United States. 3. United States~Intellectual life. I. Title.

PA78.U6 K67 1998   98-73004
480/.7/073~dc21   CIP

Published in the United States by:

    ISI Books
    Post Office Box 4431
    Wilmington, DE 19807-0431

Manufactured in the United States of America

Matri carissimae

Away with him, away with him! He speaks Latin.

—*Henry VI, Part Two*

CONTENTS

Section III. CONTEMPORARY CHRONICLES:
ROLE MODELS AND POPULAR CULTURE

ACKNOWLEDGEMENTS

The author would like to thank the editors of *Chronicles* (Rockford Institute), *Academic Questions* (National Association of Scholars), *Modern Age* (Intercollegiate Studies Institute), and the old *Southern Partisan* for commissioning the original versions of several chapters of this book. Parts of other chapters have been delivered before audiences as talks sponsored by the John Randolph Club, the Philadelphia Society, the National Association of Scholars, the Intercollegiate Studies Institute, and the Zenith Boosters Club of Kansas City. All have been revised and corrected. Chapters I, IV, VI, VII, XXI, XXII, the Epilogue, and the Appendix are original to this volume. I am especially grateful to the editors associated with ISI Books who skillfully guided this project to completion.

INTRODUCTION

Innovation and constant change are the distinctive traits of modern life. They often seem the one certainty in this age. 150 years ago a young man with a doctorate in Classical Philology from the University of Jena (1841) said nearly the same thing about his own age: "Constant revolutionizing of production, uninterrupted disturbance of all social conditions, everlasting uncertainty and agitation distinguish this epoch from all earlier ones. All fixed, fast-frozen relations, with their train of ancient and venerable prejudices and opinions, are swept away, all new-formed ones become antiquated before they can ossify."

So wrote Karl Marx in 1848, the year he penned the *Communist Manifesto*. As he knew from his classical studies, he was not the first person to feel this way. The confused middle-class hero of Aristophanes' *Clouds* (423 B.C.), confronting the world of his day, cried out, "Zeus has been overthrown and Whirl, constant swirling change, is King!" But *what* to say about this situation? How to come to grips with it? Marx's answer was, "All that is solid melts into air, all that is holy is profaned, and man is at last compelled to face with sober senses, his real conditions of life, and his relations with his kind."

Now, I agree wholeheartedly with Marx regarding the evanescence of the old ways, but I beg to differ with him on the actual conditions of human life and our relations with one another. The treasured things of the past, what seemed once "solid" and "holy" in bygone years, are indeed fading fast, but have they disappeared altogether? And if they have, is that a good thing? I contend it is not.

The purpose of this book is to suggest that the permanent things embedded in tradition are good things for human life, and that they have not yet entirely vanished from the Western landscape. Into the shadows of the gloom, admittedly real and growing, an occasional ray of light may shine, illuminating the vitality of tradition and the possibility of its restoration. Tradition is a hardy thing.

Though animated by a belief in the historically-grounded principles of classical republicanism—including personal responsibility and limited self-government—this book is not a work of political theory. Rather, it is a series of essays about the health and vitality of America's classical and Christian traditions, the errors of the current powers that be, and, most important, the ways in which creativity and order might be restored in spite of these powers. The book, as is fitting given the intellectual tradition that animates it, is both analytical and prescriptive.

By way of introduction to the central theme of the book, tradition, let me point out one important but often neglected fact, namely that everyone knows at least one tradition through personal experience: the tradition of one's native language. Traditions we value, whether science or Christianity, are best experienced in the tongues that helped form them. When Martin Luther called upon the councillors of the German cities to found and maintain Christian schools, he wanted the schools to teach the Sacred Tongues: Hebrew, Greek, and Latin. "The languages are the sheath in which the sword of the Spirit is lodged," he explained. And he was right. Thomas Jefferson, John Stuart Mill, and Albert Jay Nock, men committed to the traditions of self-rule and science, insisted on instruction in the classical languages. Ronald Knox, a wise and witty Catholic priest, when asked to perform a baptism in the vernacular, responded with what his biographer Evelyn Waugh described as "uncharacteristic acerbity": "The baby does not understand English and the Devil knows Latin."

The mental infrastructure of our English society is founded on the vocabulary and syntax of Greek and Latin. Serious discourse in English, on law, medicine, and politics, in particular, depends heavily on words borrowed from Greek and Latin, and for that reason alone the study of the classical languages is important. But there is a more important reason. Studying the ancient tongues allows us to hear our ancestors talking and thinking. We cannot return to their day and age; we can, however, still share their education. We can read the books they read and think again the thoughts that excited or outraged them. "The communication of the dead is tongued with fire beyond the language of the living," Eliot wrote. These are lines of communication we need to keep open.

We talk of creativity and the future, but we ignore the discipline of learning the rudiments of the past. I maintain that the past is our most important source of creativity. True creativity is always the acquisition of the old in order to fashion beautiful and meaningful things for the present. If we wish not to be a culture marked by servility, a terrible intellectual and moral error born in the absence of creativity, we must conserve the past. Tradition is, as the philosopher Josef Pieper viewed it, a challenge.

If we drop the baton of tradition while handing it to the next generation, we will be able to reckon the statistics: the number of jobs lost to other countries, of broken homes, of victims of drug addiction or physical violence. The root causes of these ills are moral and spiritual—we are not dealing just with drugs, but with incontinence, not just with unemployment, but with ignorance and, sometimes, disloyalty. To defeat them we must use words they and their Master recognize all too well: *Vade retro, Satana!* He will understand. Father Knox was right. The Devil knows Latin.

Man is intellectually nearsighted. He needs occasionally to clean his glasses of the dust that accumulates on them from carelessness and intellectual pollution. When he does so, he can see a stream of wisdom from the past, from contemporary wise men, and even from many still healthy sections of our popular culture. What follows is the record of one contemporary American's efforts to keep his glasses clean and clear.

E. Christian Kopff
Boulder, Colorado

Section I

Civilization as Narrative

Chapter I

TRADITION AND THE LUNATICS

In *The Poet and the Lunatics*, G. K. Chesterton's poet Gabriel Gale meets a brilliant scientist devoted to the cause of emancipation from tradition and social convention one evening at an informal gathering. Gale and the scientist are discussing with a few friends the scientist's philosophy when Gale realizes that the scientist is mad. The poet rushes everybody away from the house just before the scientist blows it sky-high. Gale later explains to his bewildered friends that his suspicions were alerted by seeing three goldfish gasping desperately in a pool of water on a table in the library. In accordance with his philosophy, the scientist had liberated them from their bowl.

The struggle between Gabriel Gale and the mad scientist represents the most important contest of our age. According to Nietzsche, archetypical modern, "The man who diverges from tradition is a victim; the man who does not is a slave." Aristotle saw things differently. "To live according to your country's way of life is not slavery," he wrote in his great reflections on *Politics*; "It is salvation." The divide could not be wider, and therefore, the enmity could not be more serious between those who side with Nietzsche and those who agree with Aristotle.

The intellectual leaders of our age stand with Nietzsche. Like Nietzsche, they feel that if they can only free themselves from the trammels of tradition in religion, science, art, and politics, true fulfillment will be theirs. For them tradition is merely memorizing what others have accomplished. Fulfillment, in their eyes, comes to those who have rejected the past, the handed-down, the socially constructed, in order to enter into a reality that is individualistic, innovative, and free. There is nothing innovative and free, however, in flopping about on a table in a pool of water. Tradition is not a cage. It is the goldfish bowl that keeps us alive.

Tradition is an everyday reality. Languages are traditions learned by each generation from the preceding one and then taught to the next, more or less successfully. Our religions, which preserve our contact with the transcendent, are Sacred Traditions. There are also secular traditions like science, history, and self-rule that provide the basis for European civilization and the American way of life.

All of these traditions, sacred and secular, are ancient. Science, for instance, began in the sixth century B.C., on the coast of Asia Minor, in a successful mercantile emporium called

Miletus. A man named Thales started talking about the world as a rational system, comprehensible to human minds, without including the gods in his explanations. For instance, he explained that earthquakes are due to giant waves in the ocean on which the earth rested, and not to the will of Poseidon, the Greek god of earthquakes and the sea. He even suggested that everything in the world started out as water.

What happened next was unusual. Another Milesian, Anaximander, accepted Thales' rather unlikely presuppositions: that the world is rational and can be understood by humans, that you can make sense of it without bringing in the gods, that the multiplicity of the world can be reduced to a single element. But he rejected the notion that the many different things of this world all come from one of the elements we know. The basis of our world must be different from any one element, though capable of producing them all. So Anaximander hypothesized that the known elements of our world developed out of an unknown element, which he called the Boundless or Infinite. He accepted some of Thales' basic presuppositions, subjected those ideas to critical analysis, and then added his own contribution.

Finally, he taught all this to someone else.

This is how tradition works. The first step is handing down the deposit. Then comes the critical evaluation of what was learned. Both steps are necessary for a truly humane assimilation of the past. Then, but only then, some gifted spirit may achieve a creative response that continues and renews the tradition. And after that, we begin again: teaching, learning, absorbing, criticizing, creating.

Anaximander's pupil, Anaximenes, responded to him as he had responded to Thales. Accepting as a given the rather unlikely notion of the world as a closed system, rational and comprehensible, he objected that Anaximander had provided no mechanism by which the Boundless could turn into the other elements. He went looking for such a mechanism and noticed that when you opened your mouth wide and exhaled, the air felt hot on your hand, but if you pursed your lips and blew, the air felt cold. He decided that the basic element was air and it changed into the others by condensation and rarefaction.

Many things have changed since the sixth century B.C. We now look for a Grand Unified Theory, not a single element. Many generations have made contributions, so that modern science looks as little like Milesian philosophy as a grown man looks like the baby he once was. When, however, John Barrow began his book *The World within the World* (1988) with a list of "traditional unspoken assumptions on which modern science is based," the first two were: "1. The Universe is ordered. 2. The Universe is logical." These two presuppositions go back to the Milesians. His third assumption, "The Universe is mathematical," goes back to Pythagoras, who lived at the end of the sixth century, and was added to the scientific tradition by Plato in the fourth century.

A similar story could be told about history, democracy, and even Christianity. Most people understand that in order to participate in science students need a long and rigorous education. Few people think this about religion and democracy, and I am puzzled by this as was Socrates. Even about science, there is an idea that it is a species of tag-team wrestling, where the participant needs to be in touch with only the previous generation to play. Creative people want to *do* science, not waste their time studying past mistakes. The fundamental presuppositions of science have not changed, however, since the sixth century B.C., so studying the history of science is not a waste of time. The long story of how brilliant minds have tried out different strategies all with the same end in mind, understanding the cosmos, is not irrelevant. It may, in fact, lead to some important new discoveries.

Take Werner Heisenberg, who propounded the Uncertainty Principle in Quantum Physics. As a student in the early years of the twentieth century, he was fascinated by the discoveries and theories of recent physicists like Max Planck and Albert Einstein. How, Heisenberg wondered, could light be sometimes a ray and sometimes a particle? This observation did not seem to fit the theory of physical atomism, itself the descendent of an ancient theory, that formed the basis of eighteenth and nineteenth century science. Heisenberg's father, however, had insisted that his son receive a solid classical education. Inducted into the militia after the end of World War I, young Heisenberg passed his free time by reading Plato's *Timaeus*, a work on the structure of the physical world, written in very difficult Greek of the fourth century B.C. Heisenberg found that Plato rejected physical atomism and looked upon matter as a mathematical construct. For Heisenberg this insight was an epiphany. Once he stopped trying to make light fit into the confines of physical atomism and thought about it in the language of mathematics, Heisenberg began to understand the new physics. As Galileo, another great reader of Plato, had put it, "The book of Nature is written in the language of mathematics." Heisenberg was not a Platonist. Heisenberg's thinking became creative, however, when he stepped out of the confines of his own age and attached himself to the tradition of science, stretching out over the millennia from Athens to Munich—and which is still alive in our own universities today!

I once heard a college administrator, who had been a lively and popular teacher in his salad days, tell a group of alumni that we teachers were not very good role models. Instead of preparing students for innovation, we spend our time indoctrinating them about the achievements of the past. This administrator was blind to what his success as a teacher and a scholar, now distant by many years, shows that he once knew. Creativity is possible only as the final stage in a long, rigorous absorption of the teachings and discoveries of the past. The last thing we need for the future of our country or of our young people is one more lunatic smashing goldfish bowls in order to free the goldfish.

If these reflections sound like an appeal to a conservative revival, it is because I believe in the creativity of conservatism. Much of the conservative revival of our day is devoted to salvaging the Roosevelt regime by modifying some of its more irresponsible financial traits. This is the "temperate conservatism" condemned by T. S. Eliot, clinging to what exists in defiance of morality and common sense. The conservatism I favor is concerned with first principles. These first principles are not spun out of thin air but rather discovered in history. One of the chief guardians of classical studies in the United States, Basil Lanneau Gildersleeve—of whom we shall learn more in chapter nine—expressed it well near the beginning of his great commentary on the Greek lyric poet, Pindar: "Large historical views are not always entertained by the cleverest minds, ancient and modern, transatlantic and cisatlantic; and the annals of politics, of literature, of thought, have shown that out of the depths of crass conservatism and proverbial sluggishness come, not by any miracle, but by the process of accumulated force, some of the finest intelligences, some of the greatest powers, of political, literary, and especially of religious life."

If this general line of thinking is valid, and I think that it is, then it is imperative for us to remember the history of our finest achievements and to retell the story to successive generations. Our society, our religion, and our science are historical growths. Human fulfillment, which cannot be realized without society, religion, and science, therefore requires nourishment from the past. Our very future, which is born of our past, demands it. Most people understand this instinctively. Authoritative sources today, however, promise us not the creative acquisition of the past, but simple innovation. We fish need to tell these lunatics that the goldfish bowl suits us just fine.

Chapter II

LEARNING TO TELL YOUR STORY

A healthy person's life forms an Aristotelian narrative; it has a beginning, middle, and end. The story will include success as well as failure, tragedy as well as comedy, high emotion as well as bathos, but it will nonetheless possess a coherence, the variegated strains of the narrative united at the stable center of the tale, the person. Indeed, anyone who cannot explain how his situation of today relates to his deeds of yesterday will not be able to understand the connection between the self he once was and his present self. He will be an alienated man. Moreover, each individual life is a part of larger wholes—family, profession, nation, civilization—in the midst of which the narrative of that life is lived out. The healthy individual, therefore, must be able to recount not only the individual story, the story of his self, but also the narrative of each of those larger wholes, in which that self finds itself, or else collapse into the *anomie* which Durkheim described and so much of modern literature portrays.

Learning to tell the stories of the larger wholes to which we belong is initially the responsibility of the family, and subsequently the responsibility of the schools also. Too often, however, today's educational system fails to lead children to a stage where they can tell the story of their nation and civilization as a coherent narrative. Traditional education, however was successful in this enterprise. Concentrating on Greek, Latin, and mathematics, traditional educators not only trained the minds of their students for careful reading and thinking, but they also introduced students to an enormous amount of myth, literature, and history—in other words, to the corporate side of their narratives. Even when the details of language and computation disappeared, as they often did, the stories remained and provided the basis for meaningful lives and productive societies.

Denied these stories by the present education system, students become like the anti-heroes of modern novels: people trapped in a world they cannot understand, bit players in a drama whose basic themes remain a mystery to them. The abolition of Latin and Greek effectively severed an entire culture from the stories that constituted, or should have constituted, its mental infrastructure. It is little wonder that many elite Americans often find Franz Kafka more appealing than Samuel Johnson. Their lives have become simply absurd.

The problem began at the close of the nineteenth century,

when people began seeking an education that would not be so time-consuming and so inaccessible to the less intelligent. The study of important texts written in challenging foreign languages was to be replaced by the reading of the same texts translated into English—in a word, the Great Books. Young people were to read the Great Books as a means of getting introduced to the narrative that their own lives were to continue but without having to pay the price their elders paid. It was civilization on the cheap.

Now, there is a measure of usefulness in this dime-store approach to education. First, even in translation the great works are difficult to read and difficult to teach. Today's students have little experience reading books that stretch them, that demand much of them, and teachers teaching contemporary books rarely demand much in the way of challenges, so the Great Books are by their nature an intellectual stimulant to both students and educators. Moreover, through the Great Books students can glimpse aspects of the universal human condition and learn how, consequently, the difficulties involved in ethical decisions and political judgments of the present hour have significance beyond it. The Great Books can, in other words, present to the student humanity in broad terms without, as is often the case today, serving up the simple emotivism of humanitarianism.

At the same time, the Great Books bring to light the differences between old and new cultures as few other contemporary approaches can. The poet Solon, for instance, helped found the Athenian democracy in the sixth century B.C. and left us poems about his political and ethical struggles. He wrote about the problem of injustice in ways that are very close to what young people feel today. Yet he is satisfied if Zeus, allowing an evildoer to escape without punishment, chastises his family instead. How different this idea of justice is from the one today's students find acceptable! But students must learn, and the Great Books can teach them, to understand how a man like Solon can be wise and good and still diverge from their own notions of right and wrong. (Some day the student may see the movie *Godfather II* and understand better than if he had not read Solon that the guilty may be more severely punished by the loss of family than by a judicial verdict, even in our own day.)

The Great Books may also teach students much about how conflicting visions of the world can encounter one another in genuine discussion. We argue about so many issues in today's world: abortion, feminism, justice. Frequently, those debates end in a *cul-de-sac* because we are arguing from different premises and even out of different traditions. There are, however, a few works of literature or philosophy that confront other traditions in a manner that allows a real discussion to take place. In his dialogues, Plato, for instance, has Socrates confront his enemies, the Sophists—the ideologues of the triumphant fifth-century Athenian democracy—and later make them part of his solution to the crisis of the *polis*. (At the time Plato wrote, the *polis*, rooted in the older Homeric vision of a warrior-based and hierarchical society, had been under attack by democratic forces.) Reading works like Plato's dialogues is essential if we are to find our way out of the current morass of disagreement; for in them we can gain an understanding of how to engage in discussions of great weight with aplomb.

The Great Books program also has the benefit of instructing students how tradition works. Virgil's great Roman epic, the *Aeneid*, was written under the Emperor Augustus in the first century B.C. We often teach it as a rewriting or modernization of Homer's Greek epics, the *Iliad* and *Odyssey*, which were composed in the eighth century B.C. In fact, Virgil had many other sources for his most brilliant creation. He went to the Greek poet Apollonius of Rhodes, author of a poem on the Argonauts written in Alexandria, Egypt, in the third century B.C. Apollonius had created a Medea in love with Jason, an affair which helped Virgil imagine the love of Queen Dido for his hero, Aeneas. Virgil even borrowed an Amazon from archaic Greek epic for his Italian Amazon, Camilla. In other words, Virgil in the age of Augustus was responding not just to Homer, 800 years before, but to the entire Greek epic tradition as it had developed over the centuries and in many lands. Virgil can teach us by example how one culture may respond positively to another, thus gaining strength and wisdom without losing its distinctiveness.

Turn now to Augustine, writing hundreds of years later, in the fourth century A.D. He builds on Virgil's accomplishments by adding the insights of the Hebrew prophets and of Jesus and Paul to the vision of Greece and the civilization of Rome. Most noteworthy among his many writings are his *Confessions* and *The City of God*. These examples, properly taught, may demonstrate to a student that originality does not necessarily mean the rejection of old forms, rather their careful assimilation. In sum, the Great Books may begin to produce in the student that sure mark of intellectual maturity, the recognition that tradition is a fruitful thing, not a lifeless, dry assortment of historical detritus.

Notwithstanding these benefits of the Great Books approach, there are flaws in it.

Today, the great majority of teachers of Great Books cannot read them in their original languages. It is disturbing that so few find anything wrong with this situation, for even the best translations are only crutches. They help us to introduce the worlds of Homer and Sappho and Aristophanes, of Virgil and Augustine, of Dante and the *Beowulf*-poet, to students who otherwise might never know of them. We must not, however, delude ourselves or our students into thinking that translated texts replace the originals. To be sure, no class in the Great Books can dwell on the linguistic intricacies of the original texts, but every course should pause at some point to bring home to the student some sense of what only direct contact with the original text can reveal.

Let me take an example from my teacher Richard Lattimore's translation of Sappho's great prayer to Aphrodite. In this poem, Sappho is in love and asks Aphrodite to make her beloved fall in love with her in return. She recalls the last time she prayed to Aphrodite; the goddess then had appeared to her and (now I quote Lattimore):

> asked me what affliction was on me, why I
> called thus upon you,
> what beyond all else I would have befall my
> tortured heart: "Whom then would you have Persuasion
> force to serve desire in your heart?"

Lattimore makes these lines a straightforward statement of passion, but in the original Greek, as Sir Denys Page has pointed out, Aphrodite's statements to Sappho repeat a word that means "again" or "this time" three times, a term Lattimore omits: "She asked me what was wrong with me this time and why I was calling on her again.... Whom this time am I to persuade to enlist as your lover?" The passion that causes Sappho to call on the goddess of love is not her first amour, and Aphrodite's statements near the end of the poem make it plain that it will not be her last. There is more than one way to read and interpret this poem. It may be an artless outpouring of a young girl's heart, or it may be a witty and distanced portrait of emotion. But only the teacher who has access to the original Greek will be able to present the class with these options and so stretch the student's appreciation of the possible range of lyric verse.

Some will say that if we apply my standards it will be impossible to find teachers for Great Books courses. After all, Greek for Homer and Plato, Latin for Virgil, Hebrew for Genesis, Italian for Dante?! I can only answer in the words of John Henry Newman ("The Tamworth Reading Room"): "I cannot help that; I never said I could. I am not a politician; I am proposing no measures, but exposing a fallacy, and resisting a pretence." The humanities will never recover the status they deserve until they are taught according to the highest standards. I certainly do not believe that knowledge of the original languages of the books teachers present in translation is enough to make a successful teacher, but I do think that it is a *sine qua non* for good teaching. And, by the by, the teacher who sets out to fulfill this language requirement will experience an increase in his self-respect as well as his humility—things in short supply in today's teachers of the humanities.

Another charge against the Great Books approach is more serious than that it unwittingly renders its practitioners susceptible to errors of translation. The change from a curriculum based on learning Greek, Latin, and mathematics to one centered on students' reading a list of great works in translation ("the Canon") is part of an historical development only one stage of which was the jettisoning of the classical language. When Paul Shorey, Professor of Greek at the University of Chicago, examined the Great Books curriculum in his *Assault on Humanism* (1917), he predicted that the replacement of ancient languages with works in translation was merely the first step towards the elimination of Western civilization from the curriculum. "Greek and Latin have become mere symbols and pretexts. They [The advocates of reform] are as contemptuous of Dante, Shakespeare, Milton, Racine, Burke, John Stuart Mill, Tennyson, Alexander Hamilton, or Lowell as of Homer, Sophocles, Virgil, or Horace. They will wipe the slate clean of everything that antedates Darwin's *Descent of Man*." Shorey was a prophet. Getting rid of Latin and Greek has meant, over time, that the entire Western intellectual tradition, which of course includes works written in English and other modern languages, has disappeared from the university curriculum. The rapid decline of Western education since the elimination of the classical languages from the university curriculum confirms Shorey's prediction, made more than 80 years ago.

Just how far the decay has affected the Great Books movement can be seen in the history of Clifton Fadiman's *Lifetime Reading Plan*, a popular presentation of the Great Books way of thinking that began as an article in *This Week* magazine (April 12, 1959) and developed into a popular book (first edition,

1960). "The Plan," Fadiman explained, " is designed to fill our minds, slowly, gradually, under no compulsion, with what the greatest writers of our Western tradition have thought, felt, and imagined.... We will know how we got the ideas by which we unconsciously live." The Plan was limited to books from the Western tradition. "We are Western men," Fadiman went on to explain. "Up to almost yesterday our minds were molded by Western ideas and images, plus those supplied by the Bible. A hundred years from now this may no longer be true. But it is true today; and this book is for now. Besides, to familiarize ourselves with the Western tradition whose children we are is a prospect big enough for any ordinary lifetime." Fadiman gives a few other reasons for his decision, including his own lack of expertise and his literary appraisal. "The Eastern classics I have read (I confess this with some embarrassment) simply light no fire inside me.... I have tried Lady Murasaki and the *Koran* and the *Arabian Nights* and the *Bhagavad-Gita* and the *Upanishads* and *All Men are Brothers* and perhaps a dozen other Eastern classics. Unable to read them with much pleasure, I cannot write about them with much honesty."

It did not take a hundred years for the situation to change, however. In 1997 *The New Lifetime Reading Plan* was published with John S. Major explaining why it now included books which lit no fire inside Clifton Fadiman:

As recently as a decade ago it was reasonable to construct a program of guided reading that included only works in the Western tradition, while acknowledging that a time might come when a shrinking world, and improvements in various communications media, would make familiarity with all of the world's literary traditions a requirement for the well-educated and well-read person. The time came sooner than one might have expected. For an American in the last decade of the twentieth century, the 'global village' is a reality, the world having been shrunk by jet aircraft, by communications satellites, by instantaneous television news from everywhere, and the Internet, to the extent that, in a sense, nothing is foreign to anyone's experience. Moreover, the United States, from its origins a nation of immigrants, has been enriched anew in recent years by fresh arrivals from all over the world, one consequence of this being that, as a people, our cultural roots have become more diverse than ever before. Because our country is now more profoundly multicultural than ever before, and also because it is to everyone's personal advantage to cast as wide a net as possible in harvesting the world's cultural riches, the works suggested in *The New Lifetime Reading Plan* now include Lady Murasaki along with Miss Austen, Tanizaki cheek-by-jowl with Faulkner, Ssu-ma Ch'ien as well as Thucydides.

The argument for deserting the traditional Western curriculum of Greek, Latin, and mathematics was straightforward. The curriculum was too difficult for many people, perhaps for most people. The argument for deserting a curriculum based on the canon of the Western Great Books is also straightforward. The curriculum is inadequate and restrictive in a world united by the global influence of Western technology based on Western science and the widespread popularity of Western-style political systems. (In the latter case representative democracy is always privileged, although on the face of it Marxist dictatorship rules just as impressive a number of people, and both developed out of the Western political tradition.) I can see the argument, which I do not advocate, that the global influence of Western technology, science, and political systems implies that other cultures should give up their traditions and learn Western traditions. I can see no logic, however, in Americans deserting Western culture at a time when they see the fruits of that culture desired all over the world.

Take the example of technology. Using tools is a cultural universal. All humans do it and as far as we can tell, using tools is one of the defining characteristics of *homo sapiens*. Without Western science to help them, the Egyptians built the Pyramids—as impressive an accomplishment as the Apollo Space Program, which did depend on Western science. If the American people want to give up on aeronautics, biochemistry, and computers and build pyramids, then they need to spend less time on Western traditions and more time learning Egyptian traditions. In fact, Americans want a future with a heavy dose of the benefits of technology, science, and representative government—all the fruits of the tree of Western culture. If we want the advantages of Western culture, we need to immerse ourselves and our children in the languages, literatures, and ideas that shaped that culture.

Mastering the text of Lady Murasaki is a worthwhile enterprise, as worthwhile as any other. It truly makes sense, however, only in the context of learning Japanese culture. The same is true of serious study of the *Bhagavad-Gita* and the *Upanishads*, or the *Koran* and the *Arabian Nights*. Studying them only makes sense as part of a serious moral and intellectual effort to enter into Indian or Islamic culture. This is not the philosophy of the new multicultural Great Books curriculum, which is modeled on the ideal of wandering down the aisles of a contemporary supermarket, free to choose *ad libitum, ad infinitum*, and, finally, *ad nauseam*. Or perhaps the model is going out to dine in a city or university town. One night we can go to the Italian restaurant, the next night to a Japanese restaurant, and the next to an Indian one. Whether such a confused diet is good for the health I leave to others, but I suspect that the more authentic the food is, the less digestible such a diet will ultimately prove. I am quite sure that in the life of the mind and the soul, a diet of Dante one day, Lady Murasaki the next, and the *Mahabharata* after that will prove not only indigestible, but poisonous.

The new multicultural Great Books curriculum is not only intellectually incoherent, it is culturally incoherent. It prepares the student to participate in no one culture. It leaves the victim of such a curriculum on the outside of every culture, hungry and cold, with his nose pressed against the window, staring enviously and impotently at the riches within. Whether you are to become a Brahmin, a Samurai, or a scientist, the initiation is long and difficult. The same is true for Kshatriya or citizen. The first step in all these cases is learning the culture that provides the soil in which these different visions of human fulfillment grew. It is for this reason that those who dwell in the West must first turn to the traditions of the West. You may be able to buy the ingredients at the multicultural supermarket, but you cannot learn the art of preparing a nourishing meal. Art is a discipline rooted in a specific culture.

Chapter III

THE LATIN INVASIONS OF ENGLISH

Students need a practical education, and nothing is more practical than the study of Latin.

One reason to study this so-called "dead language" is to learn the vocabulary of English. True, of the 100 most commonly used words in English, only 10 or so come from Latin. Of all English words, however—over a million in the latest dictionaries—more than half are of Latin origin, and those of Greek origin take up much of what remains. In the Third Edition of *Bright's Old English Grammar and Reader*, edited by Frederic G. Cassidy and Richard N. Ringler, the editors wanted to make a point about English: "In sum, it should be evident that there is a considerable degree of continuity in the core of the English vocabulary between Old English times and the present." To make the point, they printed the sentence just quoted with the words of Latin origin deleted. The sentence looked as follows:

"In ___, it should be _____ that there is a _____ of _____ in the _____ of the English _____ between Old English times and the _____."

A glance shows that the sentence is incomprehensible without the Latin-derived words. The structural skeleton of most English sentences—three quarters of them—consists of articles, prepositions, and forms of the verb "to be" which come from Old English; but the meaning of the sentence, the flesh and muscle of its body, comes from the Latin words. Without the Latin words, the sentence is a frame with no picture. (Using only the Latin words, you could eventually puzzle out the authors' intention.) Cassidy and Ringler's example shows that in serious discourse in English, it is the words of Latin origin that carry the meaning.

Linguists tell us that English is a form of Low German, so how did such a thing, at first sight a rather unusual one, come about? The story is one I like to call "The Latin Invasions of English."

Julius Caesar tried to invade Britain twice in the 50s of the last century B.C. His account of those invasions is so brilliant and exciting that few readers notice that two invasions followed by two withdrawals represent defeat, not victory. It was 100 years before another Roman tried to conquer Britain, and then it was the Emperor Claudius. Claudius was not an impressive figure. He limped when he walked. He drooled when he talked.

Worst of all, he was an ancient historian, author of a history of the Etruscans. Despite the support of the Praetorian Guard, his administration seemed doomed. Then he had a brainstorm.

If you, reader, are ever the leader of a nation—prime minister, say, or president—and your popularity is sinking in the polls, follow Claudius's example: invade and conquer a small island. The examples of Lady Margaret Thatcher and President Ronald Reagan show that it is still an effective way to win lasting popularity. (The fates of President George Bush and Prime Minister John Major indicate that participating in the invasion of small nations situated on the mainland does not engender the desired effect on the populace.) Claudius did not know of the Falklands or Granada, neither of which had been discovered in his day, but from the writings of his ancestor, Julius Caesar, he had heard of Britain.

The British king whose name survives in our literature as Shakespeare's Cymbeline had just died, and his sons were fighting over the succession. The Roman army took advantage of the situation to land in Britain and win some skirmishes. Claudius showed up in time to take credit for the victory and returned to Rome as a conquering hero. He held a triumph, named his son Britannicus, and never again had to fear lack of popularity. (His wives' intriguing was something else again.)

Now, Latin-speaking Britain proved a wealthy and happy province. Roman villas spread throughout the land, and old cities prospered, while new foundations, such as Londinium, sprang up and grew. The future emperor Constantine, who hastened the Roman Empire on the road to Christianity, spent much of his youth there.

Eventually, however, the Roman Empire fell on evil days. Constantine's reforms led to a long life for part of the Empire— the East, which survived until 1453—but some limbs did have to be amputated to preserve the health of the body. One of those limbs was Britain. Roman troops were withdrawn in the early fifth century A.D., and before long German tribes began landing on Britain's shores. The Latin-speaking Celts fought back, and our stories of King Arthur have their origin in those distant days. But eventually the Germans won, and Britain became England, the land of the German-speaking Angles and Saxons.

Our beer-swilling, venison-munching, barbaric ancestors did not know much Latin; at the most a few words. Our ancestors noticed the Roman roads, *strata*, from which we get "street." (Like many Latin words, *strata* was picked up by scientists in the 19th century and so survives twice in English. Such "doublets" are far from rare. A good parallel is the chivalrous medieval word "feat" and the cold 19th-century word "fact," both descendants of the Latin *factum*.) Likewise, in their wanderings through Europe before reaching Britain, the Angles and Saxons could hardly have failed to notice the great Roman fortifications. "Wall" is the first half of Latin *vallum*. They saw the Romans drinking wine and eating cheese, and two important English words, straight from Latin *vinum* and *caseus*, were born. *Caseus*, like *strata*, has suffered from our inability to pronounce vowels purely (a defect we inherited from our Anglo-Saxon ancestors), so we say "cheese," which is not quite right. But, on the other hand, the *w* of our "wine" preserves the correct Latin pronunciation of the first sound in *vinum* long after the Romance descendents of Latin twisted the pronunciation to *v*. After the conversion of the Germans, more Latin words came into English from Christianity, including "candle" and "altar."

In 1066 the Angles and Saxons themselves were conquered by a new set of barbarians, the Normans of France, who spoke French instead of German. The conquering Normans imported a whole slew of Latin words, modified by their transition through Late Latin into French. These new words were part of the language of the conquerors, and Latin became associated with rulers. So while what a peasant works with, his "hands," is a good German word, what an aristocrat uses to enjoy the results of that work; "stomach," is a Latin word. Similarly, those filthy animals the Saxons herded for their rulers were "swine," a German word, but the delicious food made from them for the aristocracy's dinners was "pork," a good Latin word. Latin still suffers from the feeling that it is the language of an oppressive elite.

The 16th century brought the Renaissance and the Reformation and with them new inventions, new continents, and new ideas. All these new things cried out to be labeled with new words, of course, but important writers in English made a very significant decision. Instead of trying to weld together new sounds to signify all the new discoveries of their world, these writers turned their backs on the present and sought in the rich and sophisticated world of antiquity the old words to describe the new things and events.

A few examples out of a cornucopia of possibilities: How do you describe the feeling that things are getting better? When your world is a unified whole, where classes and doctrines change not, you do not need such a concept. But people in the sixteenth century felt that there had been emendation in life in general. So they picked up a Latin word for travel—"progress." The Middle Ages used the noun "progress" to describe the passage of the king from one noble house to another. 16th-century Englishmen, though, used it to describe things not just "a going" but "a going somewhere." Soon the noun "progress" was being used as a verb, "to progress," even by William Shakespeare. Before long an adjective had developed, "progressive," which Francis Bacon found useful. Then, for a variety of reasons too complex to relate here, "progress" faded away from common use in England. In the 19th century, however, the word began to be used again, particularly in the United States, and it has stayed on to this day.

Another example: How do you describe the feeling that you are getting older but also better? Sir Thomas Elyot, T. S. Eliot's distant ancestor, wrote a book on education, *The Boke named the Governour*, and while writing it he felt the need of a word to express just this thought. He considered using the word "ripe" from the plant world, but some vague linguistic instinct told him that older people would not want to be called "ripe." So he turned to the Latin word for "ripe," *maturus*, "reservying the words ripe and redy to frute and other thinges." People who got better as they grew older were "mature," and their condition was "maturity." Aging Baby Boomers can be grateful for the thoughtful Elyot and for hundreds of other writers who in the 16th and 17th centuries coined thousands of new English words out of old Latin and Greek ones. Now, all these new words did not survive, but many did, enriching our speech and allowing the genius of our language to "mature" in an orderly fashion.

The phenomenon of turning to antiquity for very old words to label quite new things may be seen for a second time in Western history in the nineteenth and twentieth centuries. That age turned to ancient Greece and Rome for the words to describe, for example, the "locomotive," the "aeroplane," "sociology," and "hermeneutics." And the process is still going as the twenty-first century dawns. We are all concerned with computers nowadays, for instance, but the word comes right out of Latin—*computo*, "I reckon." ("Compute" and "count" are another set of doublets, like "feat" and "fact.") The little flashing marker that is blinking at me as I write these words is called a *cursor*, another good Latin word, for "runner."

Our society, unlike many others, has been able to assimilate change and newness without coming apart, and that is because we have always explained development and innovation by employing concepts and words drawn from tradition. It is a typically Western thing to do, and by doing it we maintain continuity with our past and keep our balance. When we turn our backs to tradition, the risk we face is falling. Without the solid foundation of our classical heritage, modern Americans can no longer use the past to keep sane in the present. Is it any wonder life so often feels like a free-fall experience?

Chapter IV

BACK TO THE FUTURE

"Don't look back," the great baseball pitcher, Satchel Paige, said. "Something might be gaining on you." Authoritative figures, from commencement speakers to presidents of the United States, tell us year after year that we should face the future. Indeed, President Clinton's favorite rock 'n' roll song enjoins us, "Don't stop thinking about tomorrow. Yesterday's gone! Yesterday's gone!" So it may seem incredible that anybody would suggest, with a straight face, that we turn our backs on the blank screen of the future and face the past— our own, our nation's, and our civilization's. And yet that is precisely the advice that this book offers. There are, however, a number of commonsense reasons for this advice. T. S. Eliot gave one in his famous essay, "Tradition and the Individual Talent." "Someone said: 'The dead writers are remote from us because we know so much more than they did.' Precisely, and they are that which we know." In addition, C. S. Lewis pointed out that, if in our wandering we discover that we have taken the wrong path, the progressive thing to do is to turn around and go back to where we went astray. These mild and reasonable assertions should not ruffle any feathers. After all, Eliot's point is one of the key arguments for a liberal education. And Lewis is propounding nothing more than a Sunset Law for stupid ideas.

Renewal and creativity in a host of areas—artistic, political, and religious—come from returning to the sources of the traditions, not in barreling on ahead to the future. That is a fact. Here are a number of examples from the past to demonstrate it—chosen, to be sure, because I know something about them—but true nonetheless.

I shall start with the Greeks. They were not the absolute beginning of intellectual life, but ideas they had and things they did still influence the way we think and act.

During the second millennium B.C., mainland Greece was the site of an interesting civilization, which we call Mycenaean. Now, the Mycenaean Greeks possessed an attractive art, high-walled strongholds and enough gold to bury some with their leaders. At a certain stage they even conquered the exciting and attractive Minoan civilization on Crete. Then, late in the second millennium, Mycenaean culture came crashing down. Many hypotheses exist to explain the catastrophe, which also happened more or less at the same time to other near eastern cultures

(to the Hittites, for example), but the facts in all these theories
are the same. Urban life virtually disappeared from Greece for
centuries. Strongholds were deserted. Gold went missing from
burial sites. And art becomes simpler.

Scholars speak of a Dark Age. Then during the eighth century B.C. something happened. The population grew. People
started to live in cities again. These cities, feeling themselves
crowded, sent out colonists to found other settlements all over
the Mediterranean, from Marseilles to Sicily and southern Italy,
to Cyrene in North Africa, and on into the Black Sea. Archaeologists have found pots from this period with the earliest Greek
writing, which is impressive enough; but for us the beginning
of real Greek writing consists of two great epics, the *Iliad* and
Odyssey, even if those poems contain passages or even entire chapters ("books" or papyrus rolls) which come from later periods.
Although these epics were conceived and created at a time when
the Greek people were growing in numbers and expanding all
over the Mediterranean, they do not describe or even mention
the striking contemporary revivification.

Both epics talk about the distant Mycenaean past, four
hundred and more years before, in the second millennium.
Homer was well aware that things were different then. Warriors
wore bronze, not iron, as in the eighth century. People were
bigger then. Both observations are correct, whether he knew
them from oral tradition or from the bodies of heroes who had

been dug up for reburial as part of public worship. (Both Spartans and Athenians dug up and reburied the bodies of great warriors from their past. Orestes was recovered by the Spartans, and Theseus by the Athenians—just as the Venetians went after the body of St. Mark.) Sometimes Homer's reconstructions were mistaken. Homer was sure, for instance, that the heroes of the past were illiterate and was driven to fudging a story where Bellerophon is sent to a king with the written message, "Kill the bearer of this message." Greeks in the eighth century were well aware they had just adopted an alphabet from their competitors in trade, the Phoenicians, and wrongly assumed that their ancestors could not read and write. (In fact, the Mycenaeans did possess a syllabary, or signs for each syllable, even if they did not have an alphabet, or signs for each sound. We know this fact from archaeological excavations and philological research—not always done by professional archaeologists and philologists, by the way.) But for me the most interesting thing is that so much of the great literature composed during this very expansive and creative period was devoted to talking about the past—even if the eighth-century Greeks like Homer got some details of their ancestors' lives wrong.

Devotion to the past was not limited to Homer. The political leaders of the Greek world, men who were creating the new cities and founding the new colonies, did not proclaim that they were Self-made Men doing it their way. For example, the tombs of Mycenaean notables had been deserted for hundreds of years, but in the eighth century Greeks started celebrating feasts and religious ceremonies in these places—these political leaders were proud to claim descent from the nobles of the earlier civilization. Moreover, inspired by myths about a distant generation of heroes, these new Greeks told one another stories about those heroes and listened to bards like Homer sing epics about them. The early Greeks had built a civilization in the second millennium that had progressed from poverty to wealth and conquest and then had sunk back into poverty. But the Greek "comeback" culture of the first millennium did not start by ignoring the past and marching resolutely into the future in defiance of it. The new Greek civilization came from reestablishing connections with the healthy origins of its predecessor.

Of course, these Greeks learned many things from the great civilizations of the Near East, as their Mycenaean ancestors had learned from Egypt and Minoan Crete. These new Greeks also created things that had not existed before. Throughout this period, however, these Greeks insisted on their connection with the past and told stories of that past. For example, with only rare exceptions, Greek tragedy in the fifth century retells the stories of Mycenaean antiquity, not new tales. When the fifth century poet Pindar sang odes in honor of aristocratic victors in the Olympic games and other contests, he usually put in a heroic story from the past into his poems. Moreover, while they were inventing science and democracy, the new Greeks invented our conception of history. The great fifth-century historians, Herodotus and Thucydides, tell of contemporary events, but they begin from the Homeric and mythical past. In the fourth century, Plato wrote his dialogues to make sense of the fifth-century Athenian democracy and the life of his master, Socrates; into many of them he wove stories that he insists were handed down from the distant past. Modern students of Plato often ignore these "myths," but Plato, as well as Herodotus and Thucydides, did not believe in a rational analysis divorced from historical context and traditional beliefs and stories.

The same story can be told of other creative periods in the history of the West. By the late first century B.C., Rome, which had risen from a small trading city on the banks of the Tiber River to a military power dominating much of the Mediterranean, was on the verge of collapse as a consequence of internecine war and political corruption. Near the end of the century, however, the adopted son of Julius Caesar gained control of the armies after the defeat of his rivals, Antony and Cleopatra, making him a most powerful monarch indeed. But what did he do? As he wrote in his official life, the *Res Gestae*: "When I had affairs in my hands, I restored the Republic."

After proclaiming the restoration of the traditional Roman Republic, he resigned the extraordinary powers he had accumulated during years of war. The Roman Senate refused to accept the resignation and granted him instead the honorary name Augustus and then proclaimed him *Princeps* or First Man, a traditional Roman title. Augustus controlled appointments of army commanders and had veto power over senators in their capacity as rulers of the provinces. Eventually, Augustus took the power of the old Tribunes of the People on a permanent basis, but, through all his acquiring of new power, Augustus insisted that his powers simply reflected Roman traditions, not dangerous innovations.

Augustus' restored Republic clearly was not the Old Republic. Augustus boasted in the *Res Gestae* of restoring temples, but he rarely worshipped in them. He passed laws to enforce traditional family morality, but he married Livia, his last wife, the day after she had given birth to a child legally that of her previous husband. (Horace nevertheless gave her the honored Roman title of *univira*, wife of one husband, in one of his poems.)

Augustus' cynical manipulation of public opinion in the institution of the monarchy has been memorably etched in Ronald Syme's 1939 classic, *The Roman Revolution*. In the last pages, however, Syme does admit that the Augustan regime rescued the Mediterranean from a century of violence and exploitation and prepared for two hundred years of growth and prosperity. We should remember that, after the Roman Empire fell, Europe dreamed of it for a thousand years. So, was the success of this regime founded on cynical hypocrisy, or the rejuvenation that comes from a return to the sources of our culture?

We find this return to the past for strength and inspiration reoccurring again and again. The sources for Dante's great *Commedia*, while finally remaining a mystery, must include the great contemporary poetry written in Provençal and Italian. Yet when the Beatrice of the poem sends down someone to save the poet from his seemingly hopeless plight, she sends the ancient Roman poet, Virgil, not the great Provençal troubadour Arnaut Daniel. Likewise, Michelangelo spent his life attempting to restore ancient standards of greatness in art and created marvels never seen before in doing so. In northern Europe, Martin Luther wanted to restore contact with the primitive Christian tradition. The creation of German as a literary language and the establishment of the genre of the Protestant hymn were not part of his plans, but these things came from the creativity that accompanied a return to the sources.

If we think of works from the early sixteenth century that we still read today, three must be included: Thomas More's *Utopia*, Luther's *Freedom of the Christian Man*, and Machiavelli's *Prince*. The three are utterly diverse in design and intent, but all would have been inconceivable to their authors without their knowledge of the classical world and its writings. The first two were composed in Latin in styles as satisfying and differentiated as any the ancient world had known. (Luther later translated his work into German.) The third was the work of a man who spent years writing notes on the first ten books of the ancient historian Livy, a contemporary of Augustus. Machiavelli's *Discourses on the First Decade of Livy* reestablished the continuity of the ancient republican tradition with the modern world and is the essential context for a proper understanding of his *Prince.* It is also the link between the ancient idea of a free state and the ideas of the American Founders—to which we now turn.

Chapter V

THE CLASSICS, THE FOUNDING, AND AMERICAN CREATIVITY

The United States of America is linked to the ancient past by many threads: by a language that is permeated with Greek and Latin words and concepts; by the rituals and confessions of the Christian faith, which arose in the ancient world and are still practiced and affirmed by Americans every week; by the scientific practice and its world view, which began as a gleam in Thales' eye in the sixth century B.C. and which presently employs and occupies millions. Nobody really contests these facts. But the tradition of self-rule, democratic or classical republican, is another story. Were the Founders of the Republic and the Framers of the Constitution truly influenced to any significant degree by the classical past?

A number of distinguished students of America think not. Bernard Bailyn, dean of scholars of the intellectual life of the early American Republic, agrees that the Founders quoted the ancients but observes (citing Richard M. Gummere's *American Colonial Mind and the Classical Tradition* [1963]) that the same passages and the same tags appear again and again. "The classics of the ancient world," Bailyn writes, "are everywhere in the literature of the Revolution, but they are everywhere illustrative, not illuminative of thought. They contributed a vivid vocabulary but not the logic or grammar of thought, a universally respected personification but not the source of political and social beliefs."

Russell Kirk modified Bailyn's view. In his essay "What did Americans Inherit from the Ancients?" in *America's British Culture* (1993), Kirk wrote:

> In truth America's political *institutions* owe next to nothing to the ancient world—although American modes of *thinking* about politics indeed were influenced, two centuries ago, by Greek and Roman philosophers long dead.... One learns much about constitutions from reading Plato and Aristotle and Polybius... but those books could not teach the Americans very much about constitutions that might be applied practically, ...chiefly what political blunders of ancient times ought to be avoided by the Republic of the United States.... The American Framers and the early statesmen of the Republic, whether Federalists or Republicans, were no admirers of classical political structures.... Nor did ancient political theory, as distinct from institutions, often obtain American approbation. John Adams wrote that he had learned from reading Plato two things only: "First, that Franklin's ideas of exempting husbandmen and mariners, &c., from the

depredations of war, were borrowed from him; and, second, that sneezing is a cure for the hiccough."

But in serious public discourse, Adams expressed himself differently than he did in his private epistolary horseplay with Jefferson. Expounding the basis of the colonies' position in *The Letters of Novangelus* (1775), Adams rebutted claims that his positions were newfangled. "These are what are called revolution principles. They are the first principles of Aristotle and Plato, of Livy and Cicero, of Sidney, Harrington, and Locke.–The Principles of nature and eternal reason." Furthermore, in the first volume of his *Defence of the Constitutions of Government of the United States of America* (1787), which was published in plenty of time to influence the Constitutional Convention, Adams quoted and discussed Polybius extensively. Here is how Russell Kirk summarized the influence of Adams's *Defence* on the delegates to the Constitutional Convention:

> For the American constitutional delegates at Philadelphia, the most interesting feature of the Roman Republican constitution was its system of checks upon the power of men in high public authority, and its balancing of power among different public offices. The Americans had learned of these devices from the *History* of Polybius.... The actual forms of checks and balances that the Americans incorporated into their Constitution in 1787 were derived from English precedent and from American colonial experience.

Kirk's analysis may seem odd since he was an admirer of Walter Bagehot. Bagehot showed in his classic, *The English Constitution* (1867), that the English constitution is highly centralized, not divided against itself. "The efficient secret of the English Constitution may be described as the close union, the nearly complete fusion, of the executive and legislative powers. No doubt by the traditional theory, as it exists in all the books, the goodness of our constitution consists in the entire separation of the legislative and executive authorities, but in truth its merit consists in their singular approximation." In the eighteenth century the English government was run by a small coterie of noble lords. The will of the majority party in Parliament was restrained by no concept of checks and balances or even a written constitution. In the nineteenth century Bagehot boasted how rapidly and decisively a British statesman, not burdened by the limitations surrounding the American president, could move.

The colonists learned checks and balances from their native political experience, to be sure, but also from classical authors.

These facts regarding the colonial and classical past were not lost on Benjamin Franklin, who saw his plans for a highly centralized government and unicameral legislature disappearing before Adams' arguments. (Adams' *Defence* was written as an attack on Franklin's views.) At last, Franklin rose in the chambers of the Constitutional Convention to protest the constant citation of classical precedent and the doctrines of separation of powers and of checks and balances that accompanied them. "We indeed seem to feel our want of political wisdom," he said, "since we have been running about in search of it. We have gone back to the ancient history for models of government, and examined the different forms of these republics which, having been formed with the seeds of their own dissolution, now no longer exist. We have not hitherto once thought of humbly applying to the Father of lights to illuminate our understanding."

After some pious reflections, Franklin concluded by moving that the local clergy be invited to begin each day's proceedings with prayer. He was asking the delegates to ignore the lessons of the past and fabricate the new constitution from their own abstract notions, in true Enlightenment style. For Benjamin Franklin, the Father of lights taught a different lesson from the Author of history, a figure for whom he is sometimes mistaken.

Alexander Hamilton rose to object and after heated discussion a motion for adjournment was carried without a vote on the motion. The delegates went off to eat lunch and calm down. The first speaker in the afternoon session was Luther Martin of Maryland, who favored an equal representation of all states, large and small, in the Senate. In the ancient Greek Amphictyonic Council held in Delphi each of the twelve member states had two representatives, though they differed widely in size and importance. Therefore, Martin proposed that each American state should have two representatives in the Senate. James Madison rose to object. We were back to quoting the ancients! Finally, Franklin rose. "Neither ancient nor modern history can give us light," he pleaded. "As a sparrow does not fall without Divine permission, can we suppose that governments can be erected without his will? We shall, I am afraid, be disgraced by little party views. I move that we have prayers every morning."

At first no one spoke. Then adjournment was moved and hastily voted.

Franklin's motion died without a second. There is no more impressive tribute to the power of the classical tradition among the Framers of the United States Constitution. It led them to ignore their most distinguished member, Benjamin Franklin, and explains why, to this day, each state has two Senators, out of deference to the Amphictyonic Council of Ancient Delphi.

Regard for classical education was widespread among the members of the founding generation. On January 6, 1816, Thomas Jefferson wrote a letter to his state legislator, Colonel Charles Yancey. As we might expect, Jefferson's letter contained reflections of general interest on many topics, ranging in this case from the dangers of a large public debt and paper money to the advantages of beer over whiskey. Near the end of his letter Jefferson mentioned his support of the legislature's paying for roads and schools but regrets that government does such a better job building roads than maintaining schools. (How little things have changed!) He goes on to say, "If a nation expects to be ignorant and free, in a state of civilization, it expects what never was and never will be." This sentence is often quoted nowadays in support of greater tax support for America's public schools. But we know what Jefferson wanted schools to teach from his *Notes on the State of Virginia,* Query 14; public schools today, it is safe to say, do not provide that education.

According to Jefferson, the first level of education should focus on teaching students to read, write, and reckon. Children in these early years are too young to be reading the Bible, Jefferson thought, but "their memories may here be stored with the most useful facts from Grecian, Roman, European, and American history." Jefferson recommended that the next level, for children from eight to sixteen, focus on "teaching Greek, Latin, geography and the higher branches of numerical arithmetic." Jefferson made this recommendation because he had observed what has often been confirmed: that in the years before puberty children have wonderful memories and, "the learning of languages being chiefly a work of memory," schools should therefore teach "the most useful languages ancient and modern." Jefferson ranked Greek and Latin chief among these useful languages. "The learning of Greek and Latin, I am told, is going into disuse in Europe. I know not what their manners and occupations may call for: but it would be very ill-judged in us to follow their example in this instance." Now, Jefferson was no conservative. His chief commitments were to freedom and creativity, democracy, and science. He understood, however, that democracy and science exist among us as traditions with roots extending back to the ancient world. And he understood further, and more importantly, that in order for tradition to remain alive and viable, mastery of the languages that gave these traditions shape and form is required.

The Founders of the American Republic understood that their mission was to recreate in a new environment, to continue in their own way, the traditions they had inherited from the past. In *Democracy in America* Tocqueville said the United States "possessed two of the main causes of internal peace; it was a new country, but it was inhabited by a people grown old in the exercise of freedom." There is no more important insight in a work replete with important insights. The Europeans who settled in the new world had left behind none of "their ancient prejudices and manners." They brought their education with them, and, as I have said, that education was classical. They brought their political traditions with them, and they interpreted these traditions in light of the classics. (In addition, according to Jefferson, the political traditions of America owe much to the Anglo-Saxon tradition of law. In fact, for Jefferson, American freedom was a restoration on new soil of "the ancient

Saxon laws." Jefferson's plans for the University of Virginia (1819) included Anglo-Saxon prominently among the "modern," *i.e.*, non-classical languages. Jefferson's decision was not due to the newborn conservatism of a retired politician. On August 13, 1776, shortly after he penned the Declaration of Independence, he wrote to Edmund Pendleton, "Has not every restoration of the ancient Saxon laws had happy effects? Is it not better now that we return at once to that happy system of our ancestors, the wisest and most perfect ever yet devised by the wit of man?")

These views on classical culture were not idiosyncratic to Thomas Jefferson. Other founders shared these ideas—as did any number of famous men back in the mother country. When John Stuart Mill was elected honorary president of the University of St. Andrews, for example, his inaugural address (February 1, 1867) presented arguments for a university education that concentrated on science, mathematics, Greek, and Latin. Like Jefferson, Mill was no conservative. Like Jefferson he was committed to a vision of the future in which progress was defined by political self-government and by widespread use of technology derived from modern science. And, like Jefferson, Mill understood that full access to the roots of self-government and science depends on knowledge of the languages that have helped preserve them.

In 1931, two generations later, Albert Jay Nock, classicist

and journalist, delivered the Page Barbour Lectures at the University of Virginia, later published as *The Theory of Education in the United States*. A disciple of Thomas Jefferson, Nock had been the beneficiary of a Jeffersonian education, as he revealed in his classic *Memoirs of a Superfluous Man*. Nock was a libertarian, and he understood, as did Jefferson—as did nearly everybody until quite recently—that the traditions of liberty and individualism can be kept alive only by those who have worked hard to assimilate those traditions, which are originally Latin and Greek.

Nock knew that the traditions of self-government are rigorous and demanding. He would have agreed with Jefferson's letter to Colonel Yancey: "The functionaries of every government have propensities to command at will the liberty and property of their constituents." "There is no safe deposit for these," Jefferson continued, "but with the people themselves; *nor can they be safe with them without information.*"

I have added the italics at the end of the last sentence to emphasize an important fact about political and cultural freedom nearly forgotten today, namely that liberty requires knowledge. There is a corollary to this fact, no less important and likewise not remembered; and that is that the acquisition of knowledge requires work, exertion, effort. So I ask the reader: Where *did* the pleasing notion arise that liberty is a spontaneous growth, that it *will* appear without effort, as long as it is not positively suppressed by tyrant or bureaucrat?

It is hard for Americans today to accept the idea that having a creative and progressive culture means participating in demanding traditions thousands of years old. We want to believe that we did it our way. Just as we walk through our supermarkets, filing past aisle after aisle of breakfast cereals and toothpaste and choose what catches our fancy, so we want to select off the shelf our life-styles, our families, our religions, our value systems, *etc.* Getting cultured in America today is, for many, essentially another form of promiscuity.

This view of culture has roots in America. In the first generation of the Republic, the French immigrant who called himself Hector St. John de Crèvecoeur, for instance, proclaimed this easy doctrine in his famous book *Letters from an American Farmer* (1783). "What then is the American, this new man? He is an American, who, leaving behind him all his ancient prejudices and manners, receives new ones from the new mode of life he has embraced, the new government he obeys, and the new rank he holds. He becomes an American by being received in the broad lap of our great Alma Mater."

Luckily for the United States, such an easy doctrine did not prevail at the founding. It does, however, prevail today. Sadly, few Americans ever reach that sure mark of maturity, the realization that we are the beneficiaries of the past. To begin with, we did not choose our parents. Neither did we choose our first language. Nor, if that first language is English, did we choose that serious discourse in important disciplines—law, politics, ethics, the physical sciences, and the humanities—is conducted in a vocabulary heavily Latinate and generously peppered with Greek words. The fact of the matter is that we can no more choose our culture and its languages than we can our parents. A trendy academic recently urged his peers to make a careful selection among what he called our "cultural baggage." We should not deceive ourselves, however. If our culture and its traditions are baggage, we are not carrying it, or paying academic redcaps to haul it behind us. It is carrying us.

Chapter VI

FEDERALISM AND CHRISTIANITY

Nowhere has the war on tradition been so open as in the area of religious tradition.

Few will be likely to deny that federal courts in the last sixty years have restricted the free exercise of religion by the people, local communities, and the states. Here is a brief litany of cases limiting this fundamental right.

• In 1940, the Supreme Court asserted its authority to intervene in state and local decisions involving religion in *Cantwell v. Connecticut,* in which it applied the First Amendment's "establishment clause" to the states by the "incorporation doctrine." The Fourteenth Amendment forbids the states to "deny...the equal protection of the laws," but the Court applied to the states the Bill of Rights, originally intended by the First Congress to be so many limits on the power of the national government, because, as Justice Roberts wrote for the unanimous court, "The

First Amendment declares that Congress shall make no law respecting an establishment of religion or prohibiting the free exercise thereof. The Fourteenth Amendment has rendered the legislatures of the states as incompetent as Congress to enact such laws." In one stroke the Supreme Court made itself the arbiter of the free exercise of religion by the states and the people.

• In 1947, in *Everson v. Board of Education*, the Court ruled that, in Justice Black's words, "The 'establishment of religion' clause of the First Amendment means at least this. Neither a state nor the Federal Government can set up a church. Neither can pass laws which aid one religion, aid all religions, or prefer one religion over another...."

• In 1962, in *Engel v. Vitale* (1962) the Supreme Court struck down New York State's Regents' Prayer, a nondenominational prayer to be read at the start of each school day: "Almighty God, we acknowledge our dependence on Thee, and we beg Thy blessings upon us, our parents, our teachers and our country." Justice Black wrote for the six-man majority (out of seven): "There can be no doubt that New York State's prayer officially establishes the religious beliefs embodied in the Regents' prayer."

• In 1968, in *Flast v. Cohen*, the Court gave standing to any taxpayer to sue under the establishment clause in order to enjoin federal expenditures in aid of religious schools. Now, judges usually deny the power to sue to persons whose only interest in an issue is their "standing" as citizens or taxpayers. But, according to *Flast v. Cohen*, under the establishment clause a taxpayer's personal commitment or ideological obsession is enough to confer standing on him. The result of this ruling was a harassing barrage of litigation aimed at, and often successful in, discouraging the public display of religious symbols and traditions.

- In 1970, Justice Douglas in his dissent in *Walz v. Tax Commission* interpreted Everson to mean that the purpose of the establishment clause was "to keep government neutral, not only between sects, but between believers and nonbelievers"— and his interpretation has proved influential.

- In 1971, in *Lemon v. Kurtzman* the Court held that a law must satisfy three criteria to pass muster under the establishment clause (Chief Justice Burger wrote for the majority): (1) The statute or practice must have a secular legislative purpose. (2) Its principal or primary effect must be one that neither advances nor inhibits religion. (3) It must not foster an excessive government entanglement with religion.

- *Lemon* was the basis for a series of decisions overturning many American traditions. *Stone v. Graham* (1980) forbade the display of the Ten Commandments in public schools. *Lee v. Weisman* (1992) stopped a high school principal from asking a rabbi to deliver a bland, nonsectarian prayer at a public school commencement since one Deborah Weisman might feel peer pressure to stand or maintain a respectful silence during the prayer. (Robert Bork noted, "She would, of course, have had no case had the speaker advocated Communism or genocide.") In *Lynch v. Donnelly* (1984), however, the Court did allow Pawtucket, Rhode Island, to include a creche in its annual Christmas display, because the creche had been drained of all religious significance by being placed among secular items.

All of these decisions were intended to marginalize religion in American life. In his dissent to *Albington School District v. Schempp* (1963), which forbade traditional Bible readings at the start of the school day, Justice Potter Stewart wrote:

> A compulsory state educational system so structures a child's life that if religious exercises are held to be an impermissible activity in schools, religion is placed at an artificial and state-created disadvantage. Viewed in this light, permission of such exercises for those who want them is necessary if the schools are truly to be neutral in the matter of religion. And a refusal to permit religious exercises thus is seen, not as the realization of state neutrality, but rather as the establishment of the religion of secularism, or at the least, as government support of the beliefs of those who think that religious exercises should be conducted only in private.

The Court's attitude toward the relationship of church and state is opposed to that of the Founders and of the early American Republic. The First Congress that adopted the First Amendment also confirmed the Northwest Ordinance, originally passed by the Continental Congress and now reaffirmed for the new free nation. The Third Article of the Northwest Ordinance reads in part: "Religion, morality, and knowledge, being necessary to good government and the happiness of mankind, schools and the means of learning shall forever be encouraged." These are not the words of men who believed in "a wall of separation between church and state," or of neutrality "between believers and nonbelievers."

George Washington expressed the same attitude in his Farewell Address of 17 September 1796, an address read every year since then in the Congress:

> Of all the dispositions and habits which lead to political prosperity, religion and morality are indispensable supports. In vain would that man claim the tribute of patriotism who should labor to subvert these great pillars of human happiness, these firmest props of the duties of men and citizens. The mere politician, equally with the pious man, ought to respect and to cherish them. A volume could not trace all their connections with private and public felicity. Let it simply be asked where is the security for property, for reputation, for life, if the sense of religious observance desert the oaths, which are the instrument of investigation in courts of justice? And let us with caution indulge the supposition that morality can be maintained without religion. Whatever may be conceded to the influence of refined education on minds of peculiar structure, reason and experience both forbid us to expect that national morality can prevail in exclusion of religious principle.

Thomas Jefferson believed no differently. In his one book, *Notes on the State of Virginia*, he asked, "And can the liberties of a nation be thought secure when we have removed their only firm basis, a conviction in the minds of the people that their liberties are of the gift of God?"

Yankees agreed. Charles Turner told the Massachusetts ratifying convention for the United States Constitution: "Without the prevalence of Christian piety and morals, the best republican constitution can never save us from slavery and ruin."

When Alexis de Tocqueville visited the United States in the 1830s, he discovered such sentiments were shared by most Americans. "I do not know whether all Americans have a sincere faith in their religion—for who can search the human heart?—but I am certain that they hold it to be indispensable to the maintenance of republican institutions. This opinion is not peculiar to a class of citizens or to a party, but it belongs to the whole nation and to every rank of society." In *Zorach v. Clauson* (1952), a young Justice Douglas, ironically enough, wrote of his fellow Americans, "We are a religious people whose institutions presuppose a Supreme Being."

If Washington, Jefferson, and Tocqueville are correct, the success of the campaign against religion will mean the gradual disappearance of republican institutions—in Turner's words, "slavery and ruin." To predict further, the erosion and collapse of free institutions will be marked by institutional corruption, both financial and sexual, and violence against both foreigners and citizens. Increasingly the government will treat the votes of its citizens as petitions submitted to a ruler, not as commands given by rulers to their subordinates. The citizens will feel and express a growing loss of confidence in the country's institutions. A growing *anomie*, marked by an increase in crime and violence and by increased drug abuse, sexual immorality, and suicide, will be prevalent.

Sadly, this describes us perfectly. What, then, is the answer? Simple—repeal the Fourteenth Amendment. Religion will flourish, and so will the republic. If you are not convinced, think of the issue this way. Either (a) The God of the Bible is the True God, or (b) The God of the Bible does not exist. Taking these propositions one at a time we get:

(a) The God of the Bible is the True God. His rational and benevolent will has structured the universe. Acknowledging His existence and following His will can lead individuals to fulfillment and nations to a just and peaceful prosperity. But, if His will is rejected, our personal lives will be racked by meaninglessness and violence, a plight eased only by escape into drugs and pornography; and our country will disintegrate into lawlessness, tyranny, and ruin.

(b) The God of the Bible does not exist. No god exists. Humans and human society are the result of the interaction of mass and energy. But religion is a cultural universal, found in every society and traced by anthropologists to the earliest human beings, who lived some 40 thousand years ago. Religion is one with human existence and human progress. In order to destroy 40 thousand years of tradition, the government will have to become oppressive, because you just can't remove something that old without breaking a lot of things, like people, who refuse to be stripped of their illusions. The likely result of the attempt to abolish religion will be that our personal lives will be racked by meaninglessness and violence, a plight eased only by escape into drugs and pornography; and our country will disintegrate into lawlessness, tyranny, and ruin.

Whether humans were created by God or molded by evolution, a government which attacks its people's religious traditions is embarking on a suicidal kamikaze mission. To stop this attack, we need to restore America's central traditions: republican institutions and a truly federal government founded on personal responsibility, trust in the popular will, and faith in the God of the Bible.

Our American culture is so "honeycombed" (Justice Douglas' word) with religious customs and traditions that the Court has been forced into all sorts of compromises and contradictions in its attempt to do away with religious faith. Justice Rehnquist mentioned a few examples in his dissent in *Wallace v. Jaffree* (1985): "A state may lend parochial schoolchildren geography textbooks that contain maps of the United States but may not lend them maps of the United States for use in geography class; a state may lend parochial schoolchildren textbooks on American colonial history but not a film about George Washington; a state may pay for diagnostic services conducted in a parochial school, but therapeutic services must be provided in a different building."

A prize example came in *Marsh v. Chambers* (1983), a suit challenging the appointment of a paid chaplain by the Nebraska state legislature. As Justice William Brennan pointed out in dissent, the *Lemon* tests of excessive entanglement were unavoidable in the process of choosing a "suitable" chaplain who would deliver "suitable" prayers. The Court majority approved the appointment of the chaplain on the grounds that chaplains had been part of legislative precedent since the Continental Congress and the First Congress that passed the Bill of Rights. (The same First Congress also approved paid chaplains for the Army and Navy.) Justice Brennan may well have wondered at Chief Justice Burger's sudden loyalty to the doctrine of original intent and indifference to his own guidelines in the *Lemon* decision. He may even have suspected that the real reason for the judicial *volte-face* was the fact that Chief Justice Burger and the rest of the court were well aware that a case was making its way up the judicial system brought by atheists protesting the use of chaplains by the U.S. Congress and the Court did not want to rule on the issue. If the Supreme Court ever ruled that Congress could not hire chaplains to begin every day with the kind of prayer that the Court has denied public schools, the Congress might take revenge by using its Constitutional power to move the power of judicial review to another court, thereby ending at one stroke the most prestigious prerogative of the Supreme Court.

The attack on the people's free exercise of religion has created resentment from the subject population, even in liberal Boulder, Colorado. For over twenty years the city's Fairview High School held a Christmas program of seasonal music which ended with student choirs marching out of the auditorium humming "Silent Night." For choir director Ron Revier, it was "a simple, magical moment of bonding." In 1992 district administrator Lydia Swice forbade the ending because humming "Silent Night" created "a religious service atmosphere." (Notice that even the "atmosphere" of religion is too much for these people.) Revier tried to salvage his finale by laying his hands on some repulsive New Age lyrics to be sung to the music of "Silent Night" while desecrating all the song stands for. It was not enough. The day before the musical program in 1994 Queen Herod issued her decree. No singing. No humming. Better silence than "Silent Night."

So, the next night, when the program was over, the students started filing out of the auditorium in humiliating silence, providing an excellent example of freedom of religion and freedom of expression under the liberal regime. As the students filled the aisles of the auditorium, the audience rose to its feet and started singing "Silent Night." The students joined in. They filled the auditorium of Fairview High with words and music celebrating the birth of a holy infant. Glories streamed from heaven above. Heavenly hosts sang, "Hallelujah!" As a contemporary educator might phrase it, "it was a magical moment of bonding."

This small act of civil disobedience is being echoed by others all over America, because the courts have forgotten what Abraham Lincoln told Stephen Douglas in their famous debates: "In this time and this country, public sentiment is every thing. With it, nothing can fail; against it, nothing can succeed." The Supreme Court's decisions are both tyrannical, because they deny the people's right to self-rule, and also confused, because no one can guess how it will rule from one case to the next. Out of prudence the Court should retreat from its untenable position and allow states and local communities to rule themselves. Power, however, is rarely surrendered voluntarily.

So the Speaker of the House, Newt Gingrich, proposed the School Prayer Amendment: "Nothing in this Constitution shall be construed to prohibit individual or group prayer in public schools or other public institutions. No person shall be required by the United States or by any state to participate in prayer. Neither the United States nor any state shall compose the words of any prayer to be said in public schools." When that amendment failed, Representative Ernest J. Istook of Oklahoma proposed the Religious Freedom Amendment: "To secure the people's right to acknowledge God: The right to pray or acknowledge religious belief, heritage or tradition on public property, including public schools, shall not be infringed. The Government shall not compel joining in prayer, initiate or compose school prayers, discriminate against or deny a benefit on account of religion."

A couple of questions on these amendments come to mind. (1) Do we really think the Court, with its "penumbras," "emanations," "rules," and "tests," will be unable to interpret its way around the Congress' simple stratagems? (2) And more to the point, do we need more intervention from the national government? (This is not a point likely to be understood by the Speaker of the House, who, in his book *To Renew America*, called Franklin Roosevelt, "perhaps the greatest president of the Twentieth Century.")

We need not one amendment more, but one amendment fewer. Kill the Fourteenth Amendment. If the Fourteenth Amendment were repealed, the Court, losing the "incorporation doctrine," would be neutered of its power to impose its secular vision on the American people. The states and the people would regain their just powers to experiment or not to experiment with religion, to rule the lives of their fellow citizens or to leave them alone—as the states and the people saw fit. There are many reasons to repeal the Fourteenth Amendment, as Americans from liberal California governor Pete Wilson to conservative columnist Samuel Francis have seen, and the Court's tyrannical and bizarre misreading of the establishment clause is only one of them. Without that repeal, however, the Court will continue to wage its misguided war against religion in general and Christianity in particular.

Chapter VII

THE ENLIGHTENMENT PROJECT

Near the end of the fifth century B.C., Hippocrates wrote a lecture for his medical students on the island of Cos to explain to them how the study of medicine differed from the other sciences of the day. "Medicine differs from subjects like astronomy and geology, of which a man might know the truth and lecture on it, and yet neither he nor his audience would be able to judge whether it was the truth or not, because there is no sure criterion." According to the great doctor, other sciences propound theories, but medicine had developed the observational method as a way of testing theories. Hippocrates made it clear, however, that he was not the possessor of a unique insight granted to him as a guru. He was the heir of generations of experience and observation. In one important passage, he asked what difference there is between the doctor, who recommends a diet for a sick person, and a cook, who prepares a meal for healthy diners. His answer was, none. Both have assimilated the wisdom of the past, thought about it, and contributed to their specialties by means of it. It was appropriate that Geoffrey Kirk, in translating Hippocrates' lecture, changed the title from the usual "On Ancient Medicine" to "Tradition in Medicine." Hippocrates' lecture was one of the first, and remains one of the most convincing, arguments that Western science lives within a tradition and is not simply a compilation of abstract notions and individualistic speculations.

Hippocrates' lesson was understood and accepted for millennia, until the Enlightenment. In the eighteenth century, radical critiques of tradition favoring instead general principles propounded by intellectuals and applied to the world from on high began to appear. These new disciplines had the impudence to style themselves "sciences." Near the end of the nineteenth century, classical philologist Friedrich Nietzsche brilliantly turned the tables on the Enlightenment Project by demonstrating the historical and cultural bases of what had become the Tradition of Anti-Traditionalism. Advocates of both the Enlightenment Project and the Nietzschean critique dominate intellectual discussions in the late twentieth century and often engage in pitched battles, but they agree on one thing: hostility to the traditional ideas of Western intellectual life.

In our day, the lessons of Hippocrates' introductory lecture, which testify to the central thrust of the Western intellectual tradition, are often forgotten or ignored. We have thrown away over two thousand years of educational observation and experiment, exemplified in works like Quintilian's *Institutes*, Thomas Elyot's *Boke named the Governour*, Roger Ascham's *Scholemaster*, and the essays of Thomas Jefferson, John Stuart Mill, and Albert Jay Nock, in favor of an orgy of theory descended from Rousseau, who proudly proclaimed, "Let us do away with the facts. They have nothing to do with the case."

In the humanities, the situation is particularly bad. Now, many people would acknowledge that the humanities are in trouble in the United States. Who could miss the destructive nihilism inherent in contemporary literary theory? Few, however, understand that the humanities' problems began with the rejection of the ancient traditions of philology and their replacement with the abstract, unhistorical notions of the New Critics, who are often viewed, mistakenly I believe, as conservators of the Western literary canon. Today moderate liberals and responsible conservatives in the Academy want to return to the days of "a close reading of the text" advocated by the New Critics. But as Paul de Man pointed out in "The Return to Philology," it was precisely in that context that the ideals of more recent literary theory was born. De Man mentions specifically Reuben Brower's popular Humanities 6 course at Harvard, where many of the current generation of literary scholars served as graduate assistants after World War Two. De Man remembered that Brower had one rule for student papers: "They were not to make any statements that they could not support by a specific use of language that actually occurred in the text. They were asked, in other words, to begin by reading texts closely as texts and not to move at once into the general context of human experience or history." This is the Enlightenment Project applied to literature, and it led where the rejection of tradition, the "sure criterion," always leads: to a nihilistic orgy of ill-written speculation.

Recently, E. D. Hirsch has won notoriety for suggesting that all American school kids should learn certain facts about our culture, and has so earned the ire of the literary establishment. His first fall from grace, however, occurred much earlier, in 1967, when he wrote an heretical book that argued that the point of literary analysis, hermeneutics, was to understand what an author was trying to say. The repudiation of the thesis of this book, *Validity in Interpretation*, effectively marked, I believe, the end of true literary studies in the United States. There has been a drop of almost a third in the number of students of language and literature in U.S. colleges and universities since then. And why not? If Shakespeare and Chaucer are socially constructed puppets, not real authors trying to communicate with us, why spend time reading them?

A malaise similar to the one enervating the humanities has descended on the "social sciences," all of which have deep roots in the Enlightenment. Chesterton said, "Nothing fails like success." He could have been talking about the most successful Enlightenment social science, economics. For millennia, practical rules of economic activity had been employed by individuals and governments to support families, local communities, and nations. Then economics broke off from history beginning in the eighteenth century and sought universally valid, abstract principles for all manners of economic activity irrespective of historical circumstance. Economics soon found itself in the same position as Hippocrates' astronomy and geology; it had no "sure criterion." Economics, no longer operating within a sphere of practice, had become an alien science incomprehensible to the economic agents that mattered, men and women.

In 1952 Friedrich von Hayek published his classic denunciation of the misuse of theory in the social sciences, *The Counter-Revolution of Science.* Hayek noted "the essentially subjective character of all economic theory," a trait it shares with other social sciences, and lamented the role of economists in confusing the relation of theory and historical research. "Theoretical and historical work are thus logically distinct but complementary activities.... And though they have distinct tasks, neither is much use without the other" (p. 73). Would that econo-theorists had grasped this truth.

It is important to remember that the current paradigm in economics is only some two hundred years old. Its founding documents are Adam Smith's *Wealth of Nations* (1776) and David Ricardo's *Principles of Political Economy and Taxation* (1817). Its current popularity is partially due to the collapse of its recent opponents, not necessarily to the inherent superiority of its principles. Keynesianism was discredited by the "stagflations" of the 1970s, and Marxism suffered a humiliating defeat in the form of the political and social disarray of the Soviet Union. Popular in England in the nineteenth century, but no longer, and tried briefly by other nations at that time, Classical Liberalism is, however, now being tried on a global scale. If political leaders in the countries now experimenting with this ideology knew history, they might get off that yellow brick road, because, truth to tell, free trade is confronting the same problems that led to its general abandonment in the nineteenth century.

The myths propagated on the subject of free trade are many. Let me mention three which economic historians have refuted. (1) The nineteenth century was a period of free trade. (2) Free trade was typical of the United States in the nineteenth century when it achieved its status as an economic powerhouse with widespread prosperity among its citizens. (3) The Republican Party's traditions are those of free trade. (I take my examples from Paul Bairoch of the University of Geneva, *Economics and World History: Myths and Paradoxes* [Chicago, 1993] and Alfred E. Eckes, Jr., of the University of Illinois, *Opening America's Market* [Chapel Hill, 1995].)

(1) The theory of *laissez faire* developed from the work of the French Physiocrats and reached its first plateau in Adam Smith's *Wealth of Nations*. The Napoleonic Wars stifled naissant free trade policies, and even after 1815 the move towards tariff reduction was slow but steady. The key date is 1842, long after the factory system and British dominance in world trade were established. In 1842 Conservative Prime Minister Robert Peel repealed the Corn Laws, which had protected British agriculture. From then until the end of the century, Liberals dominated British trade policy, and Britain remained loyal to free trade until World War I. The British example, and the reduction in transportation costs attendant on technological progress, worked to liberalize European trade. But European-wide free trade practices only took off with the Anglo-French trade treaty of 1860. The negotiations for the treaty were conducted by English Liberal Richard Cobden. The treaty was put into effect in France by Napoleon III against the wishes of the majority of the deputies of the French *parlement*. "Between 1861 and 1866 practically all European countries entered into what is generally called the 'network of Cobden treaties'" (Bairoch, p. 23). Although Napoleon III fell in the Franco-Prussian War of 1870, his trade polices continued until 1879, when Bismarck achieved a protectionist majority in the German *Reichstag*. The success of German protectionist policies and a European economic slowdown lasting from 1881 to 1892 finally led the French to

adopt the Méline protectionist tariff in 1892. Most of Europe followed suit, except for Great Britain. In fact, although the decline in the percentage of British domination of world trade led to heavy pressure for tariff reform, England remained liberal until the Great War.

It really is not accurate, therefore, to say that the nineteenth century was a period of free trade. Britain went that route in 1842, the middle of the century, and although she remained free trade up to World War I, the rest of Europe experimented with classical liberal trade policies for some 25 years or so but had abandoned them by century's end.

(2) The United States was protectionist from its birth. Alexander Hamilton was the author of American trade policy, and in his famous "Report on Manufactures" (1791) he favored protection for infant industries. A consistent trade policy took some time to develop, until the young nation faced British dumping after the Napoleonic Wars. The English Liberal Lord Brougham was frank: "It was well worth while to incur a loss upon the first exportation, in order by the glut, to stifle in the cradle, those rising manufactures in the United States, which the war had forced into existence, contrary to the natural course of things." From 1816-1846 America was protectionist, with average tariffs ranging from 25% (1816) to 61.7% (1832). The American System of Henry Clay carried the day. From 1846-1860, however, Democratic presidents adhered to

a policy of using tariffs only for revenue purposes. Even so the average tariff in those years was about 20%.

(3) When Abraham Lincoln became the first Republican president, he immediately raised tariffs with the Morrill Tariff Act of 1861. He had the Civil War as an excuse, but Lincoln had always been, as he boasted, "a Henry Clay tariff man." "From 1860 to 1932 Republicans preached and practiced a nationalistic trade policy that was intended to develop the American market and advance the commercial interests of domestic producers and workers" (Eckes, p. 31). In 1925 Henry Cabot Lodge remarked on his dealings with President Wilson, "Upon the questions which arose in connection with the tariff,..I took... the Republican position, which I had always held, in favor of the protective tariff policy" (p. 9). As America became a major player in world trade, the argument for protection moved from Hamilton's notion of protecting infant industries to protecting the status of the American working man. "Republican trade nationalists considered the tariff a fee imposed on foreign producers for participating in the U.S. market" (Eckes, p. 33). William McKinley's major claim on the presidency was his shepherding of the McKinley tariff of 1890 through Congress. He defended it in a speech delivered in Beatrice, Kansas, during the Presidential campaign of 1892: "Free trade... invites the product of cheaper labor to this market to destroy the domestic product representing our high and better paid labor. It destroys

our factories or reduces our labor to the level of his. It increases foreign production but diminishes home production.... Open competition between high-paid American labor and poorly paid European labor will either drive out of existence American industry or lower American wages, either of which is unwise."

The *Democratic* Party, not the Republican, was the party of global free trade from the Tariff of Abominations of 1828 forward. Woodrow Wilson devoted a full chapter of his campaign speeches, published as *The New Freedom* (1913), to attacking the tariff. The Third of his Fourteen Points (January 8, 1918) favors "The removal, so far as possible, of all economic barriers and the establishment of an equality of trade conditions among all the nations consenting to the peace and associating themselves for its maintenance." Henry Cabot Lodge, a conservative and the quintessential Republican, in *The Senate and the League of Nations* (1925) commented laconically: "The third proposition was in essence for universal free trade. That was never, I believe, seriously considered by anyone." Lodge had forgotten, however, Wilson's Secretary of the Navy and the Democratic vice presidential candidate in 1920, Franklin Delano Roosevelt. As president from 1933-1945, Roosevelt worked to undermine the Hawley-Smoot tariff (which he did not dare to repeal outright) by various Reciprocal Trade Agreements Acts. These gave the president the right to negotiate tariff reductions as part of his management of foreign policy. By the Lend-Lease Bill of

1941, Congress, in giving the president wide power over trade, had essentially surrendered to the executive branch its constitutionally mandated supervision over trade under the Commerce Clause, Article I, Section 8: "Congress shall have power... To regulate commerce with foreign nations."

Presidents following Roosevelt, both Democrats and Republicans, continued his policies of encouraging free trade, a large high-taxing government, and an interventionist foreign policy. By 1955 average tariffs had been reduced about 70% below the average level of 1931-1934, although the U.S. had received only about 50% of the tariff concessions it had granted, under very un-Reciprocal Trade Agreements.

True, the Reagan administration enforced the anti-dumping legislation of 1979—unlike earlier similar measures—and so set back the Japanese invasion of the U.S. economy for a time. Voluntary Restraint Agreements protecting American industries in automobiles, computer chips, and machine tools were negotiated, and earlier protection of a number of other industries, such as textiles, was enforced. But these brave efforts could not halt the free trade tide. Abstraction, not practical reality, had come to power—and there has been no dislodging it.

How bad have things gotten as a result of free trade—a classic example of Enlightenment ideology? Not very, according to free trader Robert J. Samuelson. "Trade doesn't determine unemployment," wrote Samuelson in 1996, "because trade mainly affects a small part of the job base: manufacturing. In 1995, its share of all U.S. jobs was 16%." We need a little history, however, to interpret this statistic correctly. In the 1950s 33% of U.S. jobs were in manufacturing. In the 1970s manufacturing jobs were about 30% of all U.S. jobs. But by the late 1980s the figure was 20%. In 1995 it was 16%. By the mid-nineties, in other words, entire industries—e.g. TV, VCR, glasses' frame, and cellular phone manufacturing—had disappeared down the globalist memory hole. Even industries that managed to get and keep protection had suffered terrible losses. In the 1970s America was the number-one producer and exporter of machine tools. In the 1980s America was still strong in machine tools, with 108,000 jobs devoted to making and exporting them (the industry was saved from Japanese dumping in the second half of the 1980s by a Voluntary Restraint Agreement). By 1995, however, the number of jobs in machine tools–related jobs had dropped to a mere 58,000. All told, some 2.5 million manufacturing jobs have disappeared from the U.S. economy since 1979. *Pace* Samuelson, that is not good news.

In the teeth of these numbers, however, Samuelson sought to demonstrate American prosperity by citing increased ownership of microwaves, dishwashers, and dryers—all labor-saving devices purchased to allow both husband and wife to work. Samuelson doesn't get it. Families buy labor-saving devices *because* their members work double the time they used to, not so they can. Increased ownership of these things is not the work of prosperity, in other words, but of creeping poverty. Ross Perot likes to say that it takes two salaries today to keep a family in the middle class. He is optimistic. The American middle class is drowning in debt. In 1996 personal bankruptcies were up 25% from 1995. By year's end bankruptcies totaled over one million, a record broken in 1997.

The New York Times, however, blames the wave of bankruptcies, typical of times of economic recession, on personal irresponsibility and easy bankruptcy laws. The bankruptcy lawyers they interviewed had another story: downsizing. "Downsizing is the current theme here," said Jonathan Kohn of Newark. Jeannie Seeliger of Jersey City told the *Times*, "We have people who have lost jobs in banking, on Wall Street, you name it, every field I can think of, and it has a ripple effect." Ms. Seeliger was obviously weak on economic theory. She thinks that if you halve the percentage of U.S. jobs in manufacturing in a generation, it has no effect on employment in other fields.

Production is treated by some people as merely one factor in economic activity. Merely one factor?! Manufacturing and farming are the *only* factors that matter, because they create wealth. Production in industry and farming has shrunk in America, but the authorities tell us police costs, medical expenses, and tourism have gone up. The fallacy of counting these activities as productive was pointed out by the great liberal

Frédéric Bastiat in his essay on "The Broken Window." Repairing a window broken by a rioter spreads the existing money around, but it frustrates real productivity and creativity.

Now, previous record-setting numbers of personal bankruptcies were set during recessions, and high percentages of mothers working outside the home are historically associated with economic hard times. These facts should tell us something, shouldn't they? By standards that matter to ordinary Americans the economy is not quite as robust as the media and political elites would have us believe. The health of the American economy is measured, however, by the Gross National and Gross Domestic Products, mathematical abstractions which ignore concrete reality.

A government study, published in the *New York Times*, August 23, 1996, discovered 8.4 million people pushed out of jobs from 1993-1995. Most found new jobs, but only a third were paid their old salaries or better. Is it any wonder there is so much bankruptcy? Those not declaring bankruptcy are barely keeping their heads above the water. Another relatively minor economic downturn, like that of 1992, will send millions of the middle class into bankruptcy. Indeed, the implosion of the American middle class within the next decade, and perhaps much sooner, is a fairly safe prediction. But remember—the Gross National and Gross Domestic Products are doing just fine.

The fact of the matter is that we need to stop measuring

our national wealth by the Gross National Product, which counts hurricanes, heart attacks, and divorce as productive activities, and by the Gross Domestic Product, which counts profits made by foreign firms in America as American productivity. We must start measuring our national wealth by what our national manufacturing industries and our farmers actually produce, and we must guide our economic policy by what these manufacturers and farmers truly need. We need to return to an historical understanding of economic activity that puts the preservation of the traditions of freedom and creativity before Enlightenment abstractions.

It is not going to be easy to improve conditions for ordinary Americans. You and your wife are both working. Your consequently unsupervised children, occupied with video games and TV, are not learning the difficult subjects needed to succeed in an economy focused on cybernetics, biotechnology, and the space industry. If one of you loses his job, the new one will be at substantially lower wages. Your expenses, meanwhile, will not come down: mortgage, clothing, food, college, *etc.* As I said, it is not going to be easy, but we must try. As a first step we might try shifting the focus of education from entertaining students to teaching them to learn to read difficult and important literary and philosophical works in the original languages. Such an education prepares the mind for intellectual challenges throughout life; it does not narrowly train the individual to perform specialized tasks that will—given the whirl of progress—become outmoded. In public policy we should learn to view the social sciences as tools with which to support and enrich family, local communities, our nation, and the traditions on which these institutions rest. In sum, we need to think and act more like Hippocrates.

Chapter VIII

THE GHOST DANCE:
LIBERALISM IN CRISIS

Your house is beginning to collapse around you, the plaster drifting down to settle on the carpets, rain dripping onto the chairs and forming puddles on the table. You can do one of two things: fix the leaks and cracks or leave the house for a better one.

When your intellectual house starts to crumble, you confront the same choices. You can either start the laborious work of restoration and retouching, or walk out to find a new place to live. Today, however, many folks follow a third way. They continue to live in their collapsing houses—professing themselves pleased with the new ease of obtaining fresh water and commenting on the rug's new patterns.

The archetype of those who refuse to confront the collapse of their intellectual house is an American Indian known as the Shawnee Prophet. He began the Ghost Dance, a movement that spread during the nineteenth century among Indians in the American West. In its most virulent form it taught Indians to believe that, if they danced the Ghost Dance, they would not be harmed by the white man's bullets. This belief contributed to William Henry Harrison's victory at the battle of Tippecanoe in 1811 and the Wounded Knee Massacre of 1890.

Whether to accept new and challenging intellectual conditions brought about by the pressure of changing events or to dance the Ghost Dance is a choice many cultures have had to face. Today that choice faces American liberalism. Liberalism is drowning in cultural relativism. By denying the validity of the concept of man, liberalism has made it impossible to have a science of ethics or even to discuss ethical issues rationally. Is abortion murder or freedom of choice? How do you decide? The fact is, with no clear idea of man you can't. Passionate letters to the editor in newspapers reveal the plight of modern ethical discussion. People want to proclaim, "This is bad," but all they can say is, "I disapprove."

Alasdair MacIntyre is our most relentless tracker of this ethical crisis of the liberal regime. In *After Virtue* (1981), he recounts the history of the triumph of this "emotivism" in ethics. In *Whose Justice? Which Rationality?* (1988) he begins to point the way out of the seemingly pathless forest of ethical subjectivism. MacIntyre is not afraid to assert that the cure for the crisis is rereading the great texts of Western literature.

To be sure, others like James Fishkin have noticed the crisis of ethics. In *Beyond Subjective Morality* (1984), Fishkin examines the plight of the average educated person trying to establish a rational system of practical ethics in today's moral environment. In response to ethical questions posed by Fishkin, young people who did not simply repudiate liberalism ended up arguing on one level or another of subjectivism (what MacIntyre calls "emotivism"). That is to say, ethics for these people boiled down to personal taste. For example, Sam, one of Fishkin's subjects, had a taste for honesty, but that taste "has no more basis than his taste for T-bone steaks": "I grew up and developed a taste for honesty—that's as far as I can take it," Sam mused. "Even if I believed in, say, communism, as a political system, the way I am now, I wouldn't believe that that would give me a right to dictate to some capitalist that communism was the right system for him."

This relativism is defended by many sociology professors in the United States. Bennett M. Berger's *The Survival of a Counterculture* (1981) is good evidence of this fact. Berger, a sociology professor in southern California, made several trips to the Ranch, a countercultural commune. At one point, the inhabitants began to manifest distrust of the sociologist and his intentions, but Abe, "poet, bard, reciter of *Upanishads*," came to the rescue. Abe, Bennett writes, "pointed out to my prosecutors that two generations of social-science ethnography (he cited Benedict,

Mead, and the Lynds by name), by bringing home the message of cultural relativism to the American public, had gone far to create the atmosphere of tolerance for 'deviants,' permitting them to live, relatively unharassed, in the style that they had chosen. And rather than regard social science as their enemy, they had every reason to be grateful to it for furthering progress and enlightenment and toleration for unusual life styles.... I had never heard a more persuasive defense of our business."

That liberalism is in crisis has been clear for some time. Since the Enlightenment, liberalism has maintained a consistent antipathy to attitudes rooted in tradition and supported by prejudice, especially religious tradition and prejudice. As a political theory, liberalism is closely tied to the possibility of a secular moral culture founded on something other than the controversial religious and metaphysical ideas of any particular group within that culture.

But "independent of particular religious and metaphysical assumptions...," Fishkin asks, "can there be a nonarbitrary basis for making moral judgments? Without a positive answer to this question, liberalism must self-destruct as a coherent moral ideology." If "it would be out of bounds for the liberal state to base moral arguments—and, in particular, to base its own claims to legitimacy—on the ultimate convictions of any particular group," as Fishkin believes, then the liberal state is a logical monstrosity, and the problems it is now undergoing are a necessary and inevitable prelude to its own implosion. To state all this another way: if, in order to maintain neutrality among religious beliefs and metaphysical arguments, a liberal state must never claim any rational basis for values, then the foundational assumptions of the state undermine its very legitimacy, because any claims that can be made on behalf of the liberal state, including the claim to neutrality, are merely arbitrary. In other words, liberalism cannot even answer the question most important for it, "Why neutrality?"

Alasdair MacIntyre has accepted the conclusions of philosophical scholarship and made the natural deduction: practical ethical reasoning must take place within a definite, historically conditioned tradition—a tradition that brings with it certain religious and metaphysical assumptions or, if you prefer, prejudices.

MacIntyre does not give us another logical refutation of Rawls or Ackerman. The bibliography of logical refutations is overwhelmingly large. Just the works of clever graduate students—including junior faculty in Rawls's own department at Harvard—have given us more than enough material. Instead, MacIntyre tells the whole story of the creation of the Western tradition of theorizing about justice and practical ethics and the demise of this tradition in modernity. MacIntyre tells the story not by listing the beliefs of a long train of thinkers but by discoursing carefully on a few of the important ones: Homer, Pericles,

Thucydides (MacIntyre thinks he can distinguish the last two), Sophocles, Plato, Aristotle, Augustine, Aquinas.

The starting point of our thinking about how people act is Homer. According to MacIntyre, before the individual, there is the hero. But is the hero great because he exemplifies excellence or because he wins? In Homer, such a question cannot really be asked; the dichotomy does not exist. But in the fifth century the distinction became dangerously real. It is Plato, especially in his *Republic*, who expresses the dilemma most clearly and offers the greatest defense of excellence against mere practical success. "Plato," MacIntyre writes, "made the sophists partners in posing these problems in a way that provided... a permanent part of the framework of all subsequent discussion.... This is why the reading and the continuous rereading of the *Republic* remains indispensable to moral and cultural education."

That Plato's work has been built so essentially into the framework of our thinking was the achievement of Aristotle. For MacIntyre, Aristotle is "engaged in trying to complete Plato's work, and to correct it precisely insofar as that was necessary in order to complete it." This is a relatively new view of Aristotle. For centuries, the view was that philosophers were born into the world as either Platonists or Aristotelians—much like the "little Liberals and little Conservatives" of Gilbert and Sullivan. But this notion was undercut first by Werner Jaeger, who argued that Aristotle began intellectual life as a Platonist, and later by scholars who have shown just how similar Aristotle is to Plato's later dialogues. MacIntyre must be included in this list of debunkers of the old view of Aristotle.

By clarifying scores of problems and paradoxes present in older visions, MacIntyre puts almost every page of Aristotle into a new light. What emerges from MacIntyre's discussion is a picture of the philosopher working, not in isolation, but within a tradition. Tradition, for MacIntyre and for Aristotle, is not simply memorizing and handing down of the concepts and theories of the past, with occasional footnotes and retranslations into contemporary forms of thought or expression. Tradition is, rather, the living interaction of human minds engaged in a common task. Wendell Berry's words come to mind:

Any man's death could end the story:
his mourners, having accompanied him
to the grave through all he knew,
turn back, leaving him complete.
But this is not the story of a life.
It is the story of lives, knit together,
overlapping in succession, rising again from grave after grave.
For those who depart from it, bearing it
in their minds, the grave is a beginning....
Ended, a story is history;
it is in time, with time
lost. But if a man's life
continue in another man

then the flesh will rhyme
its part in immortal song.
By absence, he comes again.

Thinking within a tradition is creative. Indeed, it provides
the only basis for creativity, because what we call creativity in
philosophy and literature is really the humane reconciliation of
old problems with new insights. Moreover, certain traditions
have shown themselves able to respond creatively and positively
to foreign insights and visions—for example, the tradition that
extends from Homer through Plato and Aristotle to Augustine
and Aquinas. Great works of literature, from Plato's *Symposium* to Augustine's *Confessions* to Dante's *Commedia,* have been
written utilizing these foundations. Indeed, whole societies have
been built on them.

However, handing down the torch of human understanding is a risky business. Cicero made Greek thought live in great
literature in Latin. The genius of Augustine and Aquinas assimilated Christian perspectives into the living reality of Plato
and Aristotle. That tradition, also by means of humane assimilation (and genius), survived through the Middle Ages and Renaissance. But one generation may drop the project or run off
towards a *cul-de-sac.*

The Enlightenment did. Given the rapidity of change and
the wealth of new material and cultural creations of the modern period, the task of furthering the Western tradition called

for a great mind—a new Aquinas. Instead we got Hume and Kant. According to MacIntyre, rather than working to revise and revivify the great tradition, which was still alive but in need of some first-rate rethinking, these two philosophers undermined it. They posited the possibility of practical thinking valid for the individual, anywhere, anytime—not for a member of a social and intellectual community, which is what man inescapably is. (It seems to me that MacIntyre's characterization works better for the heavily Rousseauized Kant than for Hume, who was trying to do for Scotland what Cicero did for ancient Rome, namely humane assimilation of an old tradition.) Thus was established the Enlightenment vendetta against tradition and prejudice—the Enlightenment prejudice against prejudice, to paraphrase Gadamer.

MacIntyre surveys briefly the story of "the history of attempts to construct a morality for tradition-free individuals," the story of "Liberalism Transformed into a Tradition." All the attempts to construct such morality have failed. "Any hope of discovering tradition-independent standards of judgment," MacIntyre writes, "turns out to be illusory." Must we accept, then, the predicament in which liberalism has left us—that is, having no rational way to make practical ethical decisions where traditions conflict?

Not necessarily. For our society to survive, we must escape from a rapidly imploding liberalism to a tradition of ethical reasoning that can provide the basis for consensus and progress. And that is possible, if we return to our religious traditions. As Lord Devlin told us in his Maccabean Lecture in 1959, "No society has yet solved the problem of how to teach morality without religion." So we must "get religion" again if we want ethical discourse in this country.

MacIntyre sees no hope of restoring genuine ethics in the tradition of Whig conservatism, which begins with Burke and is now represented by the Neo-Conservatives and other liberals who call themselves "conservatives." For them, tradition is passive, an environment and not an *agon*. Burke's English cattle ignored the buzzing of the radical flies of summer. Unfortunately, those cattle have been stampeded by repeated stinging. So for our society to regain its health, we must take the center of our educational enterprise from the hands of the economist and the engineer and give it back to the teacher of languages and the teacher of philosophy—and to the teacher of religion.

Alasdair MacIntyre has walked out of the crumbling house of modernity—call it socialism, Marxism, liberalism, emotivism, or whatever—without even bothering to lock the door behind him. (You need not worry about the old house being left empty and forlorn. It is still crowded with Bennett Berger and John Kenneth Galbraith and a *mélange* of French and Italian Marxists and postmodernists. There are many familiar faces inside.) MacIntyre has found another dwelling, one with firm and tested foundations. True, the house has not been lived in for a while and so needs some fixing up. But in this "new" old house, things that were mere useless bric-a-brac and people who were boring or silly have again become attractive. MacIntyre has found new meaning in St. Benedict, Sophocles, Thomas Aquinas, Jane Austen, and many other people we have not thought about for a long time. In addition, the new house is not only attractive, it is beginning to feel comfortable as well—perhaps because it is not just a house but our home.

Something, however, is going on next door that sounds like a cross between a cocktail party and a political convention. If you peer over the fence, you can see clearly what these folks in the crumbling house are doing: they are dancing the Liberal Ghost Dance.

Chapter IX

THE CLASSICS AND THE TRADITIONAL LIBERAL ARTS CURRICULUM

Now, it is one thing to say that the founders of our country were classically educated and thought that form of instruction worthy enough to recommend it to posterity. It is quite another to assert that a classical education is good for Americans today. Why should *we*, who live two centuries later, want our children to have the same education as Thomas Jefferson and the rest?

When I started to think about this question, I went to the University of Colorado library and took out one of the best books in English on education, Albert Jay Nock's *Theory of Education in the United States* (1932). It is significant for our topic that, while Nock's irritable tirade, *Our Enemy, the State*, is easily available in three separate editions and is featured in most libertarian book catalogues, Nock's masterpiece, delivered as the Page-Barbour Lectures at the University of Virginia in 1931, is difficult to find and almost unknown, although in the 1950s it won the praise of a young man named William F. Buckley, Jr.

As Nock saw, there are a number of very good reasons why a liberal arts education in our society must be grounded in the study of the languages, literatures, history, and philosophy of ancient Greece and Rome. First, the cultures of the ancient Mediterranean provided the basis of American education from the Colonial and Revolutionary periods through the nineteenth century, and indeed into the first half of the twentieth. (Greek fell from its position of educational preeminence before World War I, but Latin remained a "more commonly taught language" until the 1960s.) Anyone who reads Jefferson's literary commonplace book or who peruses the correspondence of Jefferson and Adams will realize just how deeply imbued America's revolutionary leaders were with knowledge of antiquity. Carl J. Richard's *The Founders and the Classics* (1994) is only the most recent book to make this point.

As we have seen, it is often asserted that the knowledge of the ancient world possessed by our nation's Founding Fathers and the generations that followed the Revolution was superficial and consisted mainly of classical tags and *exempla*. This assertion, as I have pointed out, is a false one. But even were it true, Professor E. D. Hirsch's *Cultural Literacy* (1987) has shown how significant such shared information is in creating a common culture. The commitment of educated Americans to the classics continued from the eighteenth century through the end of the nineteenth century, as William L. Vance's two volume work on *America's Rome* (1989) has demonstrated. It is significant that the only book stolen from Thoreau's cabin on Lake Walden was his copy of Homer.

So, given this classical subtext of American history, then, not to receive a classical education is to suffer a kind of alienation not much appreciated these days but nonetheless real: an alienation from our own history.

There is a yet more important reason we should receive a classical education while in our youth. Such an education provides, in quite pure form, true education, as distinct from mere training.

This distinction between education and training is Nock's, and it is a compelling one. According to Nock, education is the study and mastery of a body of knowledge which is formative in character. Training, however, involves the learning of information aimed at the solution of an immediate problem or the accomplishment of a specific goal. Now, both training and education are important for a society. But anybody can be trained to do something. (The complexity and difficulty of the jobs will vary, of course, from short order cook to brain surgeon.) Fewer students today, however, know how to profit from education; perhaps fewer are capable. This becomes clear once the nature of education is grasped. The goal of education is to produce thoughtful people who have at their disposal a wealth of general knowledge, and who, in the light of this knowledge and with the courage to face facts, can judge matters of significance in a disinterested manner. Obviously this kind of formation is limited to the few who possess the character, the talents, and the stamina to be educated this way. A society without trained workers will not get its work done. A society without educated citizens will collapse in times of crisis and will wither away in times of ease and prosperity. Simply put, a civilization without educated citizens will cease to be civilized.

It is very important, of course, to distinguish between the classics as the foundation of education, *paideia* in Werner Jaeger's sense, and the technical scholarly study of the ancient world. The scholarly study of antiquity has been central in the history of scholarship from the early Middle Ages until today, but Americans have contributed relatively little to that study, although there have been some important exceptions.

The *Pater Philologiae* in the United States was Basil Lanneau Gildersleeve (1831-1924). Born in Charleston, South Carolina, veteran of the War between the States, professor for twenty years at the University of Virginia, Gildersleeve was appointed by President Daniel Coit Gilman (1831-1908) as the first professor, of Greek, at Johns Hopkins University in 1876. Gildersleeve helped found the American Philological Association, founded and edited *The American Journal of Philology*, composed a masterly edition of Pindar, and was a grammarian *par excellence*. He was a devoted son of the South, who, while remaining at his academic post at the University of Virginia during the school year, fought each summer in the Army of Northern Virginia, and in the 1890s wrote in the *Atlantic Monthly* "The Creed of the Old South," in which he defended the motives of his native section during the war. The generation after him included a few other figures whose contributions to scholarship are still read: Paul Shorey (1857-1934), first professor of Greek at the University of Chicago, editor of *Classical Philology* and propounder of the theory of "The Unity of Plato's Thought"; William Abbott Oldfather (1880-1945), founder of the classics library at the University of Illinois, editor of the *University of Illinois Studies in Language and Literature*, and author of some 500 articles in the great German *Realencyclopaedie*. At Harvard, William Watson Goodwin's *Syntax of the Moods and Tenses of the Greek Verb* (1889) is still in print and still used by every Greek scholar, as is John William White's *Verse of Greek Comedy* (1912), which is still indispensable in its field. George Melville Bolling (1871-1963) of the Ohio State University won much attention in Europe for his work on the text of Homer, but few American classicists know his name. Milman Parry (1902-1935) was the founder of the scientific study of "oral poetry." Trained at Berkeley and the Sorbonne, he published significant work while at Harvard and trained Albert Lord of the Department of Comparative Literature at Harvard. In the 1960s

Elroy L. Bundy of Berkeley transformed the study of Pindar, although Americans had to wait for German and Scottish scholars to point this out to them. (It may be no accident that these last three men were educated in the West and South. One occasionally comes upon American scholars at Ivy League schools who had great influence on a field, such as William Scott Ferguson (1875-1954) at Harvard or Gregory Vlastos (1907-1991) at Princeton, but they are both foreign born. (Ferguson was Canadian; Vlastos, Greek.)

Therefore, as is evident, America does have a tradition of classical scholarship, but not an overly impressive one. The following story speaks volumes. After World War II the American Philological Association published the first volume of a new critical edition of the most important ancient commentator on Virgil, the fourth-century A.D. scholar, Servius. Under the direction of the noted Ovidian, E. K. Rand, the *Harvard Servius,* as it came to be called, employed the work and scholarship of many of Harvard's most promising younger scholars. *The Journal of Roman Studies* provided a two-part review in 1948-49 by Eduard Fraenkel, a student of the great German classics scholars of the previous generation. Fraenkel's scholarship in that review devastatingly showed that one German classicist was worth more than the most prestigious classics department in the United States. The next volume of the *Harvard Servius* appeared two decades later, after Fraenkel's death, and the work, after more than fifty years in the making, has yet to be finished.

The contemporary situation of the classical scholarship in America is a mixed one. The need for a command of Greek, Latin, and German, for research tends to discourage the more frivolous types of publication now found in modern languages. Those committed to "literary theory" have been successful in winning positions, of course, but have not been able to dominate classics as they have modern language studies. Some universities have avoided nonsense by hiring foreign scholars, some quite distinguished, with sound traditional training. These scholars, however, are rarely willing to devote a career to midwifing a distinctive American philology of high quality. Classics *may* so far have been spared the serious decline in scholarly standards that mars the study of English and the modern European languages, but it is hard to see the rise of a new creative generation.

It is even more difficult to see a resurgence of interest in Jaeger's *paideia* or Nock's education. Nock said the following about the "formative character" of the study of the ancient world, words that perfectly summarize the value of *paideia*:

> The literatures of Greece and Rome comprise the longest and fullest continuous record available to us, of what the human mind has been busy about in practically every department of spiritual and social activity; every department, I think, except one—music. This record covers twenty-five hundred consecutive years of the human mind's operations in poetry, drama, law,

agriculture, philosophy, architecture, natural history, philology, rhetoric, astronomy, politics, medicine, theology, geography, everything. Hence the mind that has attentively canvassed this record is not only a disciplined mind but an *experienced* mind; a mind that instinctively views any contemporary phenomenon from the vantage point of an immensely long perspective attained through this profound and weighty experience of the human spirit's operations. If I may paraphrase the words of Emerson, this discipline brings us into the feeling of an immense longevity, and maintains us in it. You may perceive at once, I think, how different would be the view of contemporary men and things, how different the appraisal of them, the scale of values employed in their measurement, on the part of one who has undergone this discipline and on the part of one who has not. These studies, then, in a word, were regarded as formative because they are *maturing,* because they powerfully inculcate the views of life and the demands on life that are appropriate to maturity and are indeed the specific marks, the outward and visible signs, of the inward and spiritual grace of maturity.

Few students today have the desire to undergo such a maturing experience. It demands more effort than most young people are willing to make. *Paideia* is beyond them.

Paideia has few friends among members of the older generations. When the *Chronicle of Higher Education* announced in the summer of 1990 the near completion of the Plato Microfilm Library of Plato manuscripts at Yale's Sterling Library, the newspaper also announced that time had passed the project by, and that literary theory "was the route to success in the humanities." Likewise, when Donald Kagan, an ancient historian, addressed the National Association of Scholars in June 1990, he said that, as new Dean of Yale College, he planned to improve the quality of the faculty by hiring scientists. He had given up on the humanities because they had given up on formative education of Nock's sort.

Yale in past decades has had excellent scholars on its faculty—Robert Brumbaugh of Philosophy and Fred Robinson of English, to name but two—so how did we get to the awful situation of a distinguished ancient historian at one of America's most prestigious universities implying that the humanities have no future? It is a long story, but may be summarized as follows.

In the 1890s dissatisfaction with the general quality of our educated citizenry combined perniciously with a passion for egalitarian democracy to cause a revolution in our institutions of learning. Our institutions were producing truly educated citizens in increasing numbers, but, as Tocqueville said of the French Revolution, halfway down the stairs we threw ourselves out of the window in order to reach the ground more quickly. The ideals of those in charge of instructing the young began to shift from education to training in this period. First on the reformers' list of useless courses were the Latin and Greek. The twin results were more and more trained youth pouring into the workplace but fewer and fewer educated men entering the elite classes. Now, the reformers could not accomplish their goals overnight, so remnants of the old order remained. But the writing was on the wall. It was only a matter of time before all vestiges of the traditional curriculum had vanished.

The theories which governed educational reform in the United States were the theories of Rousseau, Condorcet, and the leaders of the French Revolution. These folks had their say in America during the period that followed our Tax Revolt against the English Crown, but their advice was ignored. The ideas of these ideologues returned with a vengeance in the 1890s, however, and have remained as influential ever since. It is a straight line from the introduction of the elective system in high schools and colleges, made possible by the banishment of Greek and Latin from the humanities curriculum, to the current woes of the behemoth university.

It is common among certain writers to blame the present woes of the academy on the sixties, but I can not go along with them. A return to the 1950s in the theory and practice of our schools ("Back to Basics") or of our colleges and universities would not be a salutary, conservative movement, but a last ditch effort to salvage the failures of liberalism. In 1988 in the pages of *Academic Questions*, Thomas Short, then teaching at Oberlin College, suggested that the college curriculum of the 1950s is "the traditional liberal arts curriculum." Of course, we are free to call it anything we like and to repeat the phrase over and over, in the great tradition of Lewis Carroll's Bellman, who proclaimed, "What I tell you three times, it is true." We should not deceive ourselves, however. The college curriculum of the pre-sixties era exhibited the same devotion to egalitarianism and democracy that serves as the foundation of today's radicalized academy.

Let me discuss some practical results of this egalitarianism by reference to two important areas, religion and science.

The need for proper command of ancient tongues for the clergy will probably not be disputed by most people. Martin Luther and John Calvin, the founders of Protestant Christianity, were both published scholars in a time when command of the classical tongues was essential for scholarship. Moreover, the primary task of the Protestant clergy since its founding has been the correct exegesis of the Scriptures. Those Scriptures are written in Greek and Hebrew, and the major aids in reading them are written in Latin and German.

Beginning in the middle of the nineteenth century, however, there was a determined effort, described by Ann Douglas in her *Feminization of American Culture* (1977), to turn the clergy from the intellectual rigor of exegesis and preaching to a caring service profession. This largely successful movement has had many ramifications. One effect has been the weakening of professional knowledge of the sacred tongues. I have seen clergymen who could not understand the simplest sentences of the

Greek text of the New Testament and who explicated an English translation in direct contradiction to the clear meaning of the Greek, but who, I suppose, work hard in other ways for the well being of their parishioners.

This indifference to intellectual standards has, of course, lowered expectations for the clergy, and we in the pews suffer as a consequence. When the Word is not explained in all its richness and depth, we lose touch with the Christian tradition.

Some physical scientists assert that they have no need for a liberal arts education, rooted in the study of language, but they do. Increasingly, younger scientists have lost track of the historical and ethical basis of our civilization, and that is a serious problem. Science is not spun out of the minds of individual scientists. It is, on the contrary, the achievement of a tradition of research fostered carefully and slowly for millennia. Moreover, if they lose touch with their own culture, scientists suffer from the lack of a narrative structure to frame and render their professional lives morally sensible. The effects on scientific ethics can only be devastating. For not only do the boundaries between fudging, misreporting of results, and outright fraud become smudged and unclear; the very basis of scientific research becomes occluded as well. Science is a methodologically rigorous approach to uncovering the truth of external reality. But if no truth exists, there is nothing to discover, and that will mean the end of science.

So what is to be done? How are we to improve the education of our children?

A college curriculum is based on and develops the curriculum of elementary and high schools. Children need to start with the old three R's, the use of the alphabet and numbers. The list of subjects to study after that stage, to quote Abraham Lincoln, is short and sweet, like the old lady's dance: Latin, Greek, and mathematics. Other subjects, including history, mythology, English vocabulary and syntax, even the basics of our government, can be taught in connection with those subjects. Later we may want to add the study of modern languages. Good secular schools may want to offer European languages, *e.g.*, German, French, Russian, or Italian. Religious schools, of course, will insist on Hebrew. But the principal goal of all language study must be the command of significant literary works in their native languages and an understanding of those languages' respective roles in our common culture. Oral and written proficiency have their place, but they must take a back seat to formative knowledge.

This view of language education is not a visionary fantasy. I have visited Latin classes all over America, from the Francis Scott Key Elementary School in the slums of Philadelphia to the Silverthorne Elementary School in the mountains of Colorado. Children before puberty learn languages easily, especially if the languages are related to their own language and culture.

The advantages of a classical language curriculum are enormous. Even students who do not go on to college, who do not finish high school, will have learned an enormous amount of English vocabulary, because most English words come from Latin or Greek. Although the most commonly used words in English are not of Latin origin, the vocabulary of the professions and of serious discourse on most matters is ancient in its origins. Likewise, the masterpieces of our language and important books that are being published now are written in a heavily Latinate English. So those who go on to college to study for the professions and to read the great books will be well prepared.

But what about computers and the physical sciences? Should they be part of the curriculum in the early years? The use of the computer should be learned the same way the knowledge of English should be learned, at home. School time should not be wasted on it. As for the physical sciences, my impression is that good science is based on good mathematics. If we hope to have our children comprehend science at the university level, we should teach them as much mathematics as we can. Math is the blood of science; the more they learn the better. Besides, the science that is taught in the best university science departments is usually the latest results of a professor's research, which often has moved far beyond what is found in a high school textbook. The elements of mathematics, however, will not be rendered obsolete by further research.

We talk much today of valuing creativity. If such an attitude is to be more than talk, we must face the fact that creativity is found in tradition. An educational curriculum founded on Greek and Latin gave us Jefferson and Adams, Burke and Samuel Johnson, not to mention Aquinas and Calvin, Michelangelo and Bach, Copernicus and Newton. Educators have developed curricula and texts that can be used to teach these languages at all levels, from preschool through college. The materials are out there, lying in the warehouses of the Cambridge and Oxford University Presses. We have in our hands the making of a reactionary revolution of excellence. Do we have the will to give our children their heritage?

Section II

THE GOOD, THE BAD, AND THE POSTMODERN

Chapter X

POSTMODERNISM AND THE
END OF THE HUMANITIES

For some time now, Christopher Norris has been writing on the exponents of deconstruction and other sundry versions of critical theory in the humanities. The clarity of his accounts has been a public service, since few of the philosophers and literary and cultural theorists he discusses write clearly. (The critical theorists could write well if they wanted to, of course, but that would mean giving in to the false standards of Western civilization.) For years Norris defended the leading writers of critical theory from the accusation that their deconstruction of logocentric (or, alternatively, phallogocentric) texts from Plato to Husserl trapped reader and text, and indeed the humanities as a whole, in a Skinnerian box of language from which there was no escaping; but as the years went by and as each generation, lasting about two or three years in this rapidly changing world, advanced by "deconstructing" the hidden premises of the previous generation, Norris found himself convinced that "that way madness lies." In a series of recent books, including *Truth and the Ethics of Criticism* (1994), Norris has denounced the latest maneuvers of the "Deconstructive Turn." But like Daddy Warbucks in *Mad Magazine*'s parody of Little Orphan Annie, our hero Norris may have shown up "just after the nick of time."

Norris awoke to the implications of critical theory through the Gulf War, or rather through an article on the pending Gulf War written by a leading French postmodernist, Jean Baudrillard. (See Norris' *Uncritical Theory: Postmodernism, Intellectuals and the Gulf War*, 1992). In his article, Baudrillard explained that the Iraqi invasion of Kuwait was nothing but a game played by the Powers That Be. There was no There there. Later, when the war was over, despite the massive bombings, the killing of soldiers and civilians by hostile and friendly fire, the environmental pollution, the massacre of the Kurds, the massive media cheerleading, Baudrillard wrote another article in the communist *Libération* for March 29, 1991, congratulating himself on being correct. We know, said the French intellectual, of the saturation coverage of the war by CNN, so, granted the presence of some or much disinformation, we must doubt the saturation bombing of Iraq. "If we have no practical knowledge of this war—and such knowledge is out of the question—then let us at least have the skeptical intelligence to reject the probability of all information, of all images whatever their source." Of course, he is right to point out that our knowledge of the war came from words and pictures carefully crafted to produce an effect on the uncritical. But do we really know nothing of the war? How did critical theory end up in this absurd position, Christopher Norris began to wonder?

Our troubles began early in this century, when a brilliant Swiss linguist named Ferdinand de Saussure gave some lectures, which were published after his death. In these lectures, Saussure made a simple but important point, that there is no necessary connection between the sounds of a spoken word, the sign, and what the word refers to, the signified. "Book" in English and "libro" in Italian, for instance, both refer to the same object. From this simple but true insight—the denial of which was mocked by Plato in his *Cratylus*—the postmodern theorists, however, extrapolated an intellectual nightmare. No necessary connection between signifier and signified, between spoken word and object? Then language is a closed system which has no necessary connection to anything outside itself. Words do not refer to an extra-linguistic reality. Sentences tell us nothing about the outside world. We are all trapped in the funhouse of language.

So the theorists concluded. The insanity of theorists went further than this, however. The next maneuver of the critical theorists was to jump from phonetics to semantics, and from linguistics to ontology. Not only does language not refer to outside reality, the critical theorists asserted; outside reality does not exist. Why not? Because the concept of "outside reality" is itself nothing more than a linguistic construct. This sleight of hand is refuted by, among other things, the reality of translation. The languages of Europe and the rest of the world are systems, to be sure, and thus "closed" to a certain degree; but these languages also reflect and uncover a common reality, despite their many differences. We can speak of books and dictatorship and love in many tongues, for example, and—as those who had sex with Michel Foucault learned to their cost, the fact that the English call the disease AIDS and the French call it SIDA does not make it any less communicable or deadly. Nonetheless, the critical theorists made the leap from linguistics to ontology, and the intellectual nightmare unleashed by a misappropriation of Saussure's insights began to spread.

The areas of human existence infected by the ideology of critical theory are numerous, but one of the most significant hosts for this deadly disease was the study of the humanities. As I have said in the first section of this book, in our society, as in every other, we make sense of our lives by telling our own personal stories, and, more important, by telling the stories of our local communities and our nation—the tales of our culture, in other words. The postmodern critical theorists, However, being quite consistent in their theorizing, denounced this cultural story-telling—also known as the study of the humanities—

as indoctrination, an oppressive and illusory "Meta-Narrative." If one grants their premise as they formulate it, they are right. If language has no meaningful relation to the real world, where we and our neighbors live and move and have our being, all our public stories are irrelevant. They might indeed prove interesting, entertaining, curious; but because they are senseless, like the language in which they are spoken and written, these tales have no status that render them necessary to an educational system. How could these stories be required? After all, they amount to no more than private mutterings of their authors. One begins to see why the critical theorists consider the attempt to make these tales required texts in the classroom a violation of individual freedom. To insist that the stories comprising the humanities be made compulsory learning is to insist on the arbitrary imposition of the maunderings of one private storyteller on other private storytellers, who, by definition, possess equally valid narratives.

The humanities cannot survive if those who teach them hold these ideas, because the humanities have their origin in the communal life, and they end there as well. The stories we tell become, eventually, the novels and poems we read; and we need to read these novels and poems to make sense of our own stories and to sympathize with the stories of others. Yet if the ethical and thus the corporate dimensions of the humanities are denied, humanities departments can offer only two things: a celebration of the Other—a fancy name for all those people out there whom one cannot reach—and a passion to show up the earlier generation's lack of respect for Otherness—or, to phrase it another way, to reveal the earlier generation's imposition of a meta-narrative. A feeding frenzy will, and has, ensued—the intellectual waters turned red with the Oedipodean slaughter of the textual fathers.

Examples of the inhumaneness of humanities departments are, unfortunately, plentiful. In his writings, Foucault, speaking of power/knowledge, passionately protested against the suppression of the Otherness of the mad and the criminal. Feminists like Julia Kristeva sought a fuller life for oppressed women. Other feminists argued that scientific statements about women were not factual but rather the expression of males' desire to dominate. Palestinian scholar Edward Said supposedly demonstrated that colonialism's oppression of the Easterner was not just the result of this or that corrupt regime or mistaken policy but was rooted in the West's delusion of a universally valid knowledge, a meta-narrative, which led to crass self-aggrandizement on the part of European culture. Paul de Man declared that history, and presumably biography as well, is only "a written text" and therefore a just target for deconstructive sabotage.

There are, of course, logical problems with critical theory. If we are trapped in the closed box of language, for instance, with no objective reality to correct, falsify, or confirm our notions, on what basis do we condemn or approve? The

Deconstructive Turn was good at showing up false certainties in science, progress, and other Western accomplishments. But on what basis did it condemn the West for being trapped in its own linguistic conventions? That trap is the human condition after all, is it not? Moreover, if there is no objective reality, physical or moral, how can we denounce, or even criticize, the Holocaust Revisionist for his denial of the gas chambers? Or how can we excoriate Israel for her treatment of the Palestinians? Or men for their subjugation of women?

Norris has worked hard to find evidence that some leaders have refused to follow the dogma of the sovereignty of the linguistic all the way to the end of its barren *cul-de-sac*, but without much success. The bloody ethnic conflicts of the last few years have shaken Edward Said. Julia Kristeva has declared in her recent books on the immigrant as Other that we all have an Other inside us, which we must confront and understand, and if we can do that with ourselves, why not with more conventional Others, North African immigrants or women? She has even gone so far as to declare that Nazi Germany went wrong, not through obsession with Enlightenment ideals of general humanity, but through too great an insistence on the reality of the local self and the Other. The paragraph in which she ventured this view sent shockwaves through the critical establishment. (It is interesting, is it not, that although true believers in the linguistic Iron Curtain between "reality" and language have long since moved beyond oppressive bourgeois hermeneutics of good and evil, they remain certain about one thing: the evil of Nazi Germany?) But Norris has uncovered little else in the way of a shift by the critical Mafia toward sanity.

In fact, the situation can be said to have gotten worse, not better. Derrida, for instance, early on wrote an article critical of one of the high priests of absolute alterity, Emmanuel Lévinas. In the piece, Derrida argued that we can have no communication with another except as an *alter ego*, different from us, yes, but also like us at least in some important respects. The point is well taken and true. In a later essay, however, Derrida looked more favorably upon Lévinas's demands for absolute alterity.

There is no doubt about it. Theory and its obsession with alterity has come to dominate the humanities. And this despite some unpleasant revelations about the New Left's heroes. The early promise of the first generation of critical theorists was to be fulfilled in the abolition of Platonism, capitalism, and patriarchy, and the disappearance of the subject and the author. In 1989, however, Soviet communism proved a failure, and ugly truths about the behavior of the leading figures of critical theory came to light. A diligent Belgian archivist showed, for example, that de Man had written 170 articles for the leading newspaper in Brussels during the Nazi occupation, including a major piece for the paper's anti-Jewish issue. Foucault turned from intellectual archaeology and genealogy to a study of the social construction of sex. This shift arose from no purely intellectual preoccupation, however. When he visited the homosexual bathhouses of San Francisco, Foucault indulged himself as he did not dare to do in Paris. Roland Barthes passed on, leaving for posthumous publication what his editors called his "linguistic studies" in North Africa, page after page of which recorded what little Moroccan boys said while he sodomized them.

Is there a way out for the humanities, or is everything black night and devoid of hope? Scholars in literary studies, repulsed by the direction the Modern Language Association has taken, recently founded the new Association of Literary Scholars and Critics. But, like the Back to Basics movement in elementary education, the ALSC critics seem to think that returning to the 50s can salvage the humanities. Perhaps they have forgotten that the 60s were the child of the 50s. The Association of Literary Scholars and Critics avoids words like "text" and "philology," favored words, of course, for Paul de Man and his admirers. But how does one save the humanities without the twin notions of "text" and "philology"? The trick, it seems to me, is to have the right understanding of these words, not the wrong.

And we can have such an understanding if we will but look for it. The answer lies in the rediscovery of philology in the old sense—the establishment and explanation of texts in light of the classical and Christian traditions. This kind of philology preserves contact with language and the texts and is at the same time theoretically sophisticated. As evidence that the old style philology has life, I would cite Josephine M. Guy and Ian Small's *Politics and Value in English Studies: A Discipline in Crisis?* (1993). In this work, the authors suggest that the theory and practice of editing, an enterprise with a millennia-long tradition, may provide for English studies, and the humanities as a whole, a way out of linguistic solipsism and theoretical *aporia* and usher in a return to that fruitful interaction of theory and practice that should define the humanities disciplines. I hear the third-century B.C. royal librarians of Ptolemaic Alexandria cheering already.

One bright young theorist supposedly told his friends as he lay dying of AIDS, "I die happy, because I was infected by Michel Foucault." Those words may yet be the epitaph of the humanities in the United States, but I hope not. For unlike AIDS there is a cure for postmodernism—the rich and lively and essential traditions of editing and commenting on the texts that are the basis not only of literary studies, but also of our civilization, from antiquity to the present.

Chapter XI

THE FINAL SOLUTION OF THE PHILOLOGICAL PROBLEM

With him the love of country means
Blowing it all to smithereens
And having it all made over new.
—Robert Frost

Paul de Man's life was "the classic immigrant story." He arrived in New York in 1948 from his native Belgium and worked as a clerk at the Doubleday bookstore in Grand Central Station. He met Mary McCarthy, who helped him get a job teaching French at Bard College. He fell in love with one of his students and married her. By 1955 de Man was a member of the prestigious Society of Fellows of Harvard University, and after an illustrious career in the study of literature and languages, he ended his career as Sterling Professor of Humanities at Yale. At the time of his death in 1983 de Man wielded much influence in the Yale "Hermeneutical Mafia," which had made "Deconstruction" and "Literary Theory" terms to conjure with. So the story goes.

But that is not the whole story, not nearly. In 1987 a young Belgian named Ortwin de Graef uncovered in Belgian newspapers de Man's wartime journalism, all of which was written for collaborationist papers during the Nazi occupation of de Man's native Belgium. Jacques Derrida brought the terrible news to the United States. The University of Nebraska Press agreed to publish as *Wartime Journalism: 1939-1943* the many articles that de Man had published from 1939 to 1943. The editors then asked a number of literary critics and scholars to contribute to *Responses: on Paul de Man's Wartime Journalism.*

The revelation that one of the icons of the literary Left had been strongly pro-Nazi in his youth led to a fire storm of debate over de Man, his past, and his theories. De Man's critics denounced his later literary theories as an extension of his anti-Semitic, Nazi past, while his supporters worked hard to explain away (but did not deny) that same past.

Paul Adolph Michel de Man was born in 1919 in Antwerp, the son of Robert de Man, the prosperous head of *l'Establissement de Man*, which manufactured medical instruments and X-ray equipment. His uncle, Hendrik de Man, was the head of the Belgian Workers Party and an important socialist. When the Nazis conquered Belgium in 1940, Hendrik dissolved the party and joined the collaborationist government. "For the working classes and for socialism, this collapse of a decrepit world, far from being a disaster, is a deliverance," he proclaimed. By 1941 he had changed his mind, however, left the government, and fled to Switzerland. After the war, Hendrik was convicted of collaboration and died in exile.

His nephew, young Paul de Man, a student of chemistry at the University of Brussels, wrote many articles for *Le Soir*, Belgium's most popular newspaper, which the Nazis controlled after their invasion of Belgium. He also wrote for other Nazi-controlled papers and journals. Most of his articles were on the arts, especially contemporary literature. Young Paul reviewed seriously modernist and philo-Fascist writers and argued that Germany's victory was essential to freeing the German element in Belgian society from French influence. Moreover, young Paul de Man, the Flemish nationalist, wrote an article on "Jews in Contemporary Literature" for an anti-Jewish issue of *Le Soir*. This is a pretty sordid publishing record, but not sordid enough to earn de Man a conviction for war crimes, which others on *Le Soir* earned. Perhaps de Man's reestablishment of contact with anti-Nazi Belgians, when Allied victory loomed, helped de Man. In any case, after the war, a free de Man established a publishing house with his father's money. When the house began to fail, de Man emigrated to the United States in 1948.

There is yet more to the story. De Man left behind more than an aging and broken father when he left Belgium. In 1939, de

Man had met Anaide Baraghian, the Romanian wife of fellow student Gilbert Jaeger. Anaide and Paul had fled together to the Pyrenees before the German invasion in May 1940 but later had returned to Belgium to live together. They had three children from 1941 to 1946. In 1948 de Man moved to New York. Anaide? She went to South America with their three sons. In 1949 de Man procured a position as instructor of French at Bard College, and there he soon "fell in love with" a young student, Patricia Kelley. In 1955 he made the Society of Fellows of Harvard.

Stories of de Man's complicated past eventually reached the Society of Fellows of Harvard, however, and he wrote a letter, dated January 26, 1955, to professor of comparative literature Renato Poggioli to explain.

Most of what can be checked in the letter is false. First, de Man referred to his uncle Hendrik de Man as his father. Second, de Man said he had no idea how his family business was doing. "Since 1950 or 51 I have not heard from the firm," de Man wrote. "This made me assume that things were not going well but, since I had other things on my mind, I did not give it much thought." In fact, the firm had closed, bankrupt, in 1949. Third, de Man implied in the letter that, when he entered the country in May 1948, he was already married to an American citizen. In fact, de Man did not even meet Patricia Kelley until 1949. Fourth, and most important, de Man said that he had contributed "some literary articles" to *Le Soir* in 1940 and 1941. Actually, the number of articles totaled 170. De Man also got the dates of his contributions to *Le Soir* wrong. De Man had written the pieces from 1939 to 1943, not from 1940 to 1941. De Man insisted he had ceased writing "when Nazi thoughtcontrol did no longer allow freedom of expression." Clearly he had not.

So, how did young de Man sound in his *Le Soir* articles? Consider this excerpt (the translation is mine):

> There is another reason why Germany's historical destiny, past and future, cannot leave us indifferent. We depend on it directly. First of all because there exists between Germany and Belgium a profound relationship that reveals itself through the centuries by constant political and artistic contacts. Besides that, because no one can deny the fundamental significance of Germany for the life of the West taken as a whole, we must see in that stubborn refusal to let herself be conquered more than a simple proof of national faithfulness. The entire continuity of Western civilization depends on the unity of the people who are at its center. That is why the facts that determine the course of German history touch us twice: because we are Belgians, since they affect the values we share with it and because we are Europeans, since Europe's strength depends on it. The artificial ignorance of German affairs in which we have remained during the recent past has separated us from a living source of our civilization. (*Le Soir*, March 16, 1942)

The language and clear purpose of that passage cannot be gainsaid, just as de Man's anti-Semitic article—what Jacques Derrida called the "open wound"—likewise cannot. J. Hillis Miller

tells us that the article is a defense of Jews and literary modernism against "vulgar anti-Semitism." Then one reads the article.
"Vulgar anti-Semites" think that Jews are intelligent and aggressive and run modern culture. De Man thinks, *au contraire,* that
Jews are second-rate as thinkers and as writers. If they were all
shipped off to Madagascar, Europe would lose merely some
mediocre talents. In his later academic life, de Man's colleagues
included Geoffrey Hartman, Harold Bloom, and Jacques Derrida.
Did their thinking and writing give him cause to change his
mind? We do not know. We have many statements that he did
not go around Yale making openly anti-Semitic remarks. That
silence does not quite answer the important question. Did de
Man ever change his opinion, clearly expressed in 1941, that
shipping off Jewish literary figures to "a Jewish colony isolated
from Europe would not involve, for the literary life of the West,
deplorable consequences"?

And is there a connection between de Man's wartime collaboration and his later literary theory? It is, I think, an important question. Jon Wiener, in a 1988 piece for the *Nation,*
has a simple answer. Yes. Wiener is quite sure that a number
of prominent theorists are anti-Semites and Nazis. On the sur-
face the idea perhaps sounds absurd. But Nazism, like the other
political ideologies, liberalism, communism, and fascism, was
a revolutionary movement that developed out of opposition
to traditional European values and norms. Much separates

these creeds, but this opposition is the telltale unifying thread. Gerald Graff tells us that Marxist New Historicists and feminists have seized upon Deconstruction as an essential tool in their attack on America. Perhaps former Nazis could find something useful in Deconstruction, too, in order to achieve a shared goal, the destruction of America and the European norms it preserves. In my opinion, that was the case with Paul de Man. We should give little credence to the fact that de Man did not present himself on these shores as a Nazi. An intelligent Nazi would not easily give himself away in an American university, any more than smart Communists betrayed themselves in the State Department of the 40s.

The evil genius of Deconstruction is that it allows the teacher, the transmitter of society's values, to concentrate on what is not talked about. Is Pamela frigid? Is Jim in love with Huck Finn? Why are the works of the canon permeated with Platonism, or Christianity, or patriarchy? What is the feminist perspective on Shakespeare? (I think the more important thing is Shakespeare's perspective on feminism. Read *The Taming of the Shrew*.) The teacher may spend class time, and the student may pass hours writing papers, exorcising these demons. In one essay de Man showed that Derrida falsely attributed to Rousseau a simplistic view of progress that was clearly and explicitly rejected in Rousseau's text. It does not matter, though, de Man tells us. Derrida's attitude is still the right one. The critic's blindness is essential to his genius. The point is not to enter into a sympathetic relationship with the author. That implies a false metaphysic of presence. The truest criticism is to interrupt the Great Conversation with our own concerns and to shout down, or deny tenure to, the reader, philologist, or historian who would let the authors speak for themselves. (The very idea is the sheerest logocentricity.)

The dream of the literary theorist is to concoct the final solution to our country's history—which is only "a written text," according to de Man—our literature and culture, and our religion. For its *Gauleiters*, Deconstruction is the way to free the world from "totalizing thinking," from learning from literature how to make sense of our own lives and our culture, from the delusion that wise men have distilled their wisdom in the honey of words. That is a freedom we do not need, because it is not really freedom but slavery. It is our bondage to the present, because it separates us from our past.

The only aspect of de Man's past that bothers most theorists is his contempt for Jews. And that is a terrible mark against de Man indeed. But there is more in the figure of de Man that should bother us. First, there is the question of his so-called scholarship. What are called his books are reprints of earlier essays with some new material. De Man, some will be surprised to learn, never edited a text or wrote what could be called a commentary on a work of literature. His essays typically take a small part of an author's work and discuss it from a narrow perspective. Furthermore, none of de Man's articles concerned the kind of historical and textual questions that require exacting standards of evaluation and analysis to resolve, and few of de Man's articles appeared in prestigious refereed journals. Of the essays in *Blindness and Insight*, one appeared in *Modern Language Notes*. The rest appeared first in *Feschriften*, special issues of journals, unrefereed journals, or in the *Acta* of conferences. One piece of the newly reprinted *Critical Writings* appeared first in *Comparative Literature*; the rest in foreign reviews, literary journals, or the *New York Review of Books*. A good scholar will appear in such places, of course, but he will also appear in refereed journals and presses. To top it off, de Man's style—and this is not going too far—is a mush of obfuscating jargon. (Attempting to show the influence of Sartre on de Man, Stanley Corngold wrote in 1982, "Here is Sartre's deliberate antibourgeois refusal to write well...that has proved congenial to de Man.")

The problem of de Man's lack of substantive publication is a serious one. But there are problems yet more serious, though one never hears about them, unfortunately. There is not, for instance, a single attack on de Man because he was a Quisling, because he betrayed his country for an evil ideology. The normal, healthy person loves his country as he loves his family, not because either fits into a theory, but because they are his own. If one's son fails an examination, or one's country loses a battle to Germany, one does not abandon him or repudiate it. Most Americans know what Stephen Decatur meant when he made his famous toast: "Our country, right or wrong." Just as they know what kind of man deserts his wife and children and flatters brutal dictators for self-advancement, à la Paul de Man. Given these facts of de Man's life, I believe we begin to apprehend his obsession with Rousseau, to whom de Man attributes many of his own views. It is obvious to me that Rousseau and de Man are cut from the same cloth—though Rousseau never managed to achieve de Man's triple threat status of bankrupt, deserter of his family, and Quisling.

"You must not think that living according to your country's way of life is slavery," says Aristotle; "It is salvation." This is a truth that de Man and his ilk do not understand. The mystery of tradition—that one must be happily rooted in family, in nation, in religion, in culture in order to rise above them—is lost on the critical theorists. By betraying home and family Paul de Man cut himself off from understanding great literature and, consequently, from genuine criticism. The truest critique of Paul de Man, and the deracinated mediocrities for whom he was literary *Gauleiter*, are the words John Steinbeck gave to the Chicano warrior Emiliano Zapata. "You have no wife, no woman. You have no farm, no land. You have no love. To destroy, that is your love."

The modern ideologue has turned his back on his family,

community, and nation to revel in the destruction of the cultural traditions that are built on them. They are totalitarians, despite all their chatter of ridding the world of "totalizing language." The great enemy of the antitraditional ideologues of the twentieth century has been the United States. Now as in the past, the American way of life—the life really lived by traditional Americans—represents a profound commitment to the political, ethical, and religious ideals that developed out of ancient Greece, Rome, and Israel, the traditions that formed Europe. Those traditions live on in the memory and actions of the American people. They are preserved in the books of literature, philosophy, political theory, and history that line the shelves of our libraries and homes. The key that opens those treasures to young people is as close as a teacher's enthusiasm or a parent's love. What the New Criticism did in the decades after World War II and literary theory has done over the past generation is persuade a generation of young minds that those great works are mere literary artifacts or confused propaganda for an immoral system. Paul de Man's side lost a battle in 1945. When he closed his eyes for the last time in 1983, he died in full confidence that he had won the war.

Chapter XII

SCHOLARSHIP AND BRICOLAGE

Suppose it is true that, in the wake of Deconstruction, we are living in a post-Christian age. Enlightenment liberalism and its friendly rival, postmodernism, have won the day. On what basis, then, shall we make moral decisions, create and destroy, live our lives? I suppose that, if Christianity were to disappear as the guiding moral force in the United States, another religion, perhaps Islam, would replace it. Some liberals, such as Ernest Gellner, seem to believe that we can proceed ahead with our Enlightenment tradition in order to formulate and live by another, new rationalistic morality. In *Shame and Necessity* (1993), British philosopher Bernard Williams turns to the Greek world of Homer and Attic tragedy. Like Nietzsche and Heidegger, Williams is looking to find what was right in the Greek dawn, and where Western Man took the wrong path in his long journey to the present.

Williams does many things right in his book. He devotes many pages, for instance, to attacking "progressivism," the belief that time improves all things, and that, therefore, our way of viewing reality is better than the past's way of doing so. Much of *Shame and Necessity* is really a classical version of Herbert Butterfield's famous polemic against the "Whig Interpretation of History." The specific target of *Shame and Necessity* is the great German scholar, Bruno Snell, whose *Discovery of the Mind* (1948), along with Oxfordian Eric Dodds's *The Greeks and the Irrational* (1951), dominated classical studies for a generation after World War II. (Dodds's book, like Williams', was delivered at Berkeley as part of the Sather Classical Lectures series, by the way.) It must be mentioned, of course, that Williams' book is not the first to strike at the progressivist bias in late twentieth-century classics scholarship. A key date in the assault on progressivism was the publication in 1971 of Sir Hugh Lloyd-Jones's Sather Lectures, entitled *The Justice of Zeus*. But to see how much things have changed in the past two decades, one need only compare the outrage that greeted Lloyd-Jones's brilliant book to the hosannas that have poured down on Williams'. Williams' ridicule of the view that Homer's great epics are morally primitive will help those laymen taken in by the progressivist drivel of, say, Julian Jaynes—whose *Origin of Consciousness in the Breakdown of the Bicameral Mind* assimilates the thinking of Achilles and Odysseus to the psychoses of the

Liverpool Strangler. Little in Williams' book, however, will seem new to professional classicists. Nonetheless, Williams' book does perform well on the subject of progressivism.

Second, Williams presents a masterpiece of moral thinking and careful literary analysis in "Shame and Autonomy," by far the best chapter in the book. Williams rejects the progressivist argument that shame and guilt represent two different kinds of society and human being. "Shame looks to what I am," Williams points out, and guilt has us look to others; but the idea that evolution proceeds from a primitive Shame Culture to an advanced Guilt Culture is simply not historically demonstrable. The idea also conflicts with our own feelings and observations. We see others—and if we are introspective, we feel ourselves—making decisions at times in deference to what other people will say and at other times because of our own internalized moral commitments. The ancient Greeks did the same. Evolution has nothing to do with it. Moderns wonder why there are so many more manuscripts from antiquity and the medieval world of Sophocles' *Ajax* than of Sophocles' *Antigone*. A warrior who kills himself rather than suffer humiliation (shame) seems to us on a more primitive level than a brave woman who would rather die than betray her duty to family and gods (guilt). The ancients and medievals thought otherwise. Williams helps us take Ajax, and shame, seriously again.

After making these valid points, however, Williams begins

a slide into error and faulty interpretation. Williams' important chapter on "Necessary Identities" is, for example, a much less successful one than "Shame and Autonomy." "Modern liberal thought rejects all necessary social identities...," Williams writes. "It has given itself the task of constructing a framework of social justice to control necessity and chance...." In the past, Williams has successfully employed arguments from the ancient world to make objections to this liberal ideology, which is rooted in Kantian philosophy. Williams' classic essay on "Moral Luck," for example, showed that he understood the limitations and errors of Kant's attempt to escape from the morality of "my station and its duties" into an ethic in which the individual transcends any social role, and universal human rights take precedence over the traditional and the local. *Shame and Necessity* now traces this Kantian, abstracting vision back to Descartes (correctly) and even to Plato and Aristotle (less persuasively). Nietzsche, as Williams says, "set the problem" of his inquiry. When push comes to shove, though, Williams cannot bear to relinquish the heritage of the Enlightenment.

For example, he has difficulty dealing with the apparently bizarre view, held by the ancient Greeks and explained by Aristotle, that men and women are different. Williams gives no arguments of his own or references to anybody else's when denouncing "the assumption that nature has something to tell us, in fairly unambiguous terms, about what social roles should be and how they should be distributed." But he should have, because Williams strikes a ridiculous pose in denying this assumption. Sexual role separation and male political dominance are cultural universals; they are found in every non-mythical society, including our own, and attempts to demonstrate otherwise have not held up in the court of evidence. The theories of Aristotle and others merely "save the phenomena," as good theories should. Williams regrets the continued influence of Aristotle on social theory. "The idea that gender roles are imposed by nature is alive in 'modern,' scientistic forms. In particular, the more crassly unreflective contributions of sociobiology to this subject represent little more than continuations of Aristotelian anthropology by other means." But why is Aristotle wrong, *ipso facto*? Should we not actually take a look at his theory and the evidence that backs it up before we reject it? It is a bad sign that a serious devotee of classical culture such as Williams should reject one of its best thinkers so quickly.

Williams assures us that all the ancient Greeks did not believe that the distribution of social roles reflected nature. Indeed, "in its most complete and comforting form," Williams writes, "it was almost an Aristotelian specialty." But Williams does not seriously discuss Greeks who did question traditional sex roles, like Aristophanes (for a lark) and Plato (more seriously). It would have helped his case, if he had—though not much. Euripides' Medea, for example, does complain about the sexual double standard, but she explicitly reaffirms the natural differences between men and women; her famous cry that she would rather fight three battles than give birth once is not an offer to volunteer but an assessment of relative pain and fear. And Aristophanes and Plato offer little more solid ground for Williams' unfortunate fantasy of a gender-neutral social theory than the figure of Medea does.

In sum, when he denounces Aristotle, without argument or even specific examples, Williams, despite his earlier good work, reveals all the narrowness of a philosophy severed from philological, historical, and genuine scientific research.

Williams, in his refusal to listen to the facts of social life, ends up on the same side as his old bugbear, Kant, in a common mission of salvaging the Enlightenment. Williams differs from Kant, and from Neo-Kantians like John Rawls, regarding the best way to do so, but Williams and Kant's followers share that same end. Rawls thinks a defense of the liberal regime means going back to Kant, and he has made an impressive case for that strategy. Bernard Williams, impressed by the moral and philosophical problems the Neo-Kantian strategy involves, is trying another route to a liberal social order, one suggested by Nietzsche and Heidegger: the careful investigation of a great, creative non-Christian civilization, such as Greece from the eighth to the fifth century B.C., as represented by writers from Homer to Thucydides. Williams' project is doomed to fail, however, because what the

Greeks of this period have to tell us—and it is much—does not lead directly, or even probably, to the liberal regime. Alasdair MacIntyre understood that the rejection of Kant means the rejection of the Enlightenment and, consequently, of the liberal regime, but Williams does not grasp this crucial point.

What provoked Williams to attempt such a project? His apologia near the end of the book gives a hint:

> We are in an ethical condition that lies not only beyond Christianity, but beyond its Kantian and its Hegelian legacies.... We know that the world was not made for us or we for the world, that our history tells no purposive story, and that there is no position outside the world or outside history from which we might hope to authenticate our activities.... I am not denying that the modern world is through and through different from the ancient world.... If we find things of special beauty and power in what has survived from that world, it is encouraging to think that we might move beyond marveling at them, to putting them, or bits of them, to modern uses.

This is the scholarship of *bricolage*. Williams is like a tourist who wanders out of the Holiday Inn in downtown Rome, photographs Bernini's baroque elephant, and stops for a cappuccino near the Pantheon. Williams is rummaging through the past looking for hints to solve specific problems. For him, history is the ultimate Old Curiosity Shop.

Manhandling history this way is the Enlightenment's besetting *hubris*. This is a point Alasdair MacIntyre forcefully makes in his works. In *Shame and Necessity*, Williams indeed mentions MacIntyre's thoroughly anti-Enlightenment theory that human beings think and create in traditions that of necessity must be assimilated before they can be altered, but Williams cannot, in the end, accept this. He can fiddle with bric-a-brac, but he cannot deal with coherent, long-lived practices. This is unfortunate, because, as MacIntyre demonstrates, the liberal tradition that comes from the Enlightenment, and which is dominant today, is an intellectual mess.

To put its dilemma in broad terms, the Enlightenment is the "tradition of anti-traditionalism"; it embodies, as Gadamer saw, the "prejudice against prejudice"—an impossible intellectual position to maintain in the long run. Constantly pulling out the rug from under its own intellectual feet, the Enlightenment Project cannot sustain itself. More specifically, Enlightenment minds use and misuse ideas and methods that make sense in one tradition but not in another. They view any particular tradition as so many discrete cultural elements that can be moved like game pieces. Consequently, such minds are constantly trying to transfer what cannot be transferred. It is a dangerous project. As we know, life forms cannot be transported from one environment to another without damaging them or the environment, or both. The same is true of traditions.

By the end of his book Williams is openly describing Enlightenment ideals as "social and political ideals in favor of truthfulness and the criticism of arbitrary and merely traditional power," and even as "social and political honesty." Thus, contrary to his earlier work and to his stated intention in *Shame and Necessity*, Bernard Williams ends his own Sather Lectures as a progressivist.

As the work of a talented amateur, *Shame and Necessity* is marked by brilliant insights but also by naiveté—which is not all bad—and by ignorance, which is. In dealing with classical Greek literature, for instance, Williams' ignorance of the scholarly problems of the texts he deals with, and especially of the German bibliography on these problems, is appalling. His occasional *obiter dicta* on these problems are an embarrassment. For instance, Williams' one comment on textual criticism is a permanent blot on the Sather series—a footnote suffused with arrogance and ignorance. The worst problem, however, is the author's unwillingness to admit to himself what he is doing. Like Immanuel Kant and John Rawls, Williams seeks a defense of the regime that rules his country and ours. But he misrepresents his mission, and he misrepresents the intellectual and political context of the tools he uses for his rescue operation.

Chapter XIII

MARGARET FULLER IN ROME

Oh Rome! my country! city of the soul!
The orphans of the heart must turn to thee!
—Lord Byron, *Childe Harold's Pilgrimage*

What is the greatest lost work of antiquity? Is it Arctinus' epic *Aethiopis*, which told of the battles of Achilles against Penthesilea, the Amazon Queen, and Memnon, black King of the Ethiopians? Is it Ovid's tragedy *Medea*? Or Livy's account of the Civil Wars that ended the Roman Republic? In American letters I do not suppose there is much competition with *The History of the Roman Republic of 1848-49*, by S. Margaret Fuller, alias Marchioness d'Ossoli.

In her day—she lived from 1810 to 1850—Margaret Fuller was one of the best known intellectuals in America. Her father, Massachusetts Democrat Timothy Fuller, gave his eldest child a man's education: Latin, some Greek, much German, French, and Italian. He was a demanding teacher whose lessons left her with terrifying nightmares. She grew up learned, witty, and physically plain. When she was 25 her father gave up his successful political career to write history. He promptly died of cholera and left the family for her to support. She was up to the challenge. Her famous "Conversations" attracted Bostonian ladies of culture to the Peabody sisters' bookstore where these society ladies paid twenty dollars a head to hear Margaret lecture on subjects from Goethe to Greek mythology. Afterwards the women would browse through the bookstore looking for books she had mentioned, including her own translation of Eckermann's *Conversations with Goethe*. The Conversation on Greek mythology was so popular she was persuaded to repeat it for men.

In 1840 she became the first editor of the Transcendentalists' short-lived journal *The Dial*, for which she wrote her famous feminist essay "The Great Lawsuit: Man vs. Men, Woman vs. Women." In 1845 She expanded the essay into a bestselling book, *Woman in the Nineteenth Century*. Horace Greeley lured her from Boston to write social and literary criticism for his *New York Daily Tribune*. She mingled articles on poverty, prostitution, and women's rights with praise of Emerson, Hawthorne, and Poe, and condemnation of James Russell Lowell and Henry Wadsworth Longfellow. Today these assessments are standard, but at the time her comments on Longfellow created a scandal.

Her emotional life was equally unconventional. In 1840

she lived for a while at Emerson's home. (A strange man named Henry David Thoreau was staying there, too.) Emerson and Fuller were so aroused by one another that they could not converse but retired to their respective bedrooms to pen impassioned letters back and forth. In New York she lived at Horace Greeley's house. They were close, though not romantically involved. She fell in love with a footloose immigrant, James Nathan, who, when they broke up, refused to return her love letters without suitable financial remuneration, which Margaret refused to pay—or could not.

In 1845, at age 35 she talked Greeley into financing a trip to Europe in return for 15 long articles for the *Tribune*. *Woman in the Nineteenth Century* had made her a celebrity in England, and she was invited everywhere. We finally have adequate editions of her *Tribune* articles in Larry K. Reynolds and Susan Belasco Smith's *"These Sad But Glorious Days": Dispatches from Europe* (Yale, 1991), and her letters up to 1849 in five volumes by Robert N. Hudspeth (Cornell, 1983-88). Both sources tell us of her meetings with Thomas Carlyle. She expected the sage of *Sartor Resartus*. She met a bitter, angry, though witty man and his sad, frustrated wife. Carlyle expected a frigid New England schoolmarm and discovered instead a cultured and brilliant conversationalist who knew German as well as he did. He soon tired of the wealthy Quakers who were serving as her chaperones, however. They would go on about slavery, while he wanted to talk about masters and heroes. During their debates, Margaret met Giuseppe Mazzini, intellectual leader of the fight for a united republican Italy. Many reports describe him as the most beautiful man in Europe. Dressed always in black in mourning for his country, he was vowed to celibacy until Italy was free. The early chapters of his masterpiece, *The Duties of Man*, began by addressing Italian workingmen with the words, "I have come to speak to you of your duties," and only then of their rights. Margaret warmed to him immediately. When, years later, Mazzini finished *Duties of Man*, he declared the emancipation of woman as important as that of the working class, perhaps under Margaret's influence. Neither could foresee that they were soon to meet again, in Rome.

Margaret went on to Paris and met George Sand, whose latest lover, Fréderic Chopin, was lurking about the house. Sand appears to have been an important influence on Margaret's growing radicalism. The experience was somewhat spoiled by the depressing rainy weather and Margaret's inability to converse in French with the same flair she showed in English. Margaret and the Quaker family went on to Italy, first to Naples and then to Rome.

Chesterton tells of a man who set sail to find a new country and after many adventures discovered that his new country was England, his own home. *Heureux qui comme Ulisse.* Others set sail to find a new country and, their hearts finally content,

spend the rest of their lives there, like William Wetmore Story
and his wife Evelyn. Story, the son of distinguished jurist Joseph Story, had deserted a promising career in law to move to
Rome and become a sculptor. Others return to America, like
the great sculptor of the next generation, Augustus Saint-
Gaudens, but cannot get the new country out of their hearts.
After his return Saint-Gaudens kept the faucets in his New York
studio always running, because the sound reminded him of the
fountains of Rome. Margaret, like the Storys, with whom she
became fast friends, also fell in love with Rome on first sight.
Rome is the country to which the orphans of the heart must
turn, the land of their lost content, and Margaret Fuller was
one of them.

Wandering through St. Peter's one day, she became separated from her Quaker chaperones. While searching for them,
she met Giovanni d'Ossoli. He was 25 and handsome as only
young Italian men can be, shy, and perhaps not very bright,
certainly not well educated. Margaret was cultured and inar-
ticulate in five foreign languages. Together they found their way
back to her lodgings. For the next few days he showed her around
Rome, after which it was time for Margaret and her chaperones
to continue on to Milan and Venice. In Venice, however, Margaret parted company with her escorts and headed back south.
Margaret's infatuation with Giovanni is reason enough for most
biographers. I suspect they underestimate what Rome could

mean to a woman who grew up reading Virgil and Livy. In addition, Margaret was a born newspaperwoman—as Horace Greeley knew—and in Rome was the story of a lifetime.

In 1846, a year before Margaret arrived in Italy, the aged Pontiff Gregory XVI had passed away, after inspiring some of the most brilliant anticlerical poetry ever penned, the sonnets of G. G. Belli, written in *Romanaccio*, the dialect of Rome. Even in distant London Mazzini had read *A Dog's Life*: "*Nun fa mmai ggnente er Papa, eh? nun fa ggnente?*" ("Duh Pope he don't do nutting? Whaddya mean, he don't do nutting?" and so on to detail the leisurely schedule of a contemporary Bishop of Rome.) The Consistory voted for a young moderate, Giovanni Mastai, as Pope Pius IX. Pio Nono was inspired by the Abbé Gioberti's vision of an Italy cleansed from foreign domination and reunited under papal supremacy to enjoy her old cultural hegemony in Europe. Reform would proceed hand in hand with tradition and without the need of republicanism, revolution, or communism. The new Pope granted a constitution, allowed the formation of a *Guardia civica* (George Mason's "well-regulated militia"), and even the appointment of lay ministers among his advisors. Italy rang with the cry, "*Viva Pio Nono!*"

William and Evelyn Story were amazed at the Margaret they saw in the fall of 1847. She was a changed woman, almost beautiful. The glorious fall became a rainy December, and Margaret grew depressed and the bloom faded from her cheeks as the season changed. She awoke every morning feeling sick to her stomach. George Sand had neglected to mention this aspect of living life to the full. Margaret Fuller was pregnant.

Margaret had long since rejected traditional Christianity— who among her friends had not?—but part of her was still a Puritan. She was convinced that she was going to die in childbirth. Giovanni did not share Margaret's depression. He explained that under Italian law, he could recognize his baby, give the boy (as he was sure it would be) his name, and even baptize him without marrying the mother. It is doubtful whether these legal details soothed Margaret's heart. Giovanni proposed, but she declined. Her refusal no doubt pleased the Ossoli family, which a century later still referred to Margaret as "old, ugly, Protestant, and poor." Marriage to a Protestant required a papal dispensation, and, in addition, Giovanni had joined the *Guardia civica*, a virtual proclamation of republican sympathies for which the Ossoli family blamed Margaret.

Pleading ill-health, Margaret left Rome to bear her child in seclusion, while Giovanni stayed with his regiment in Rome. Horace Greeley was not sympathetic, however. It was the spring of 1848, and all Europe was exploding with revolution. In France Louis Philippe fell, and the mob chased Metternich from Vienna. The Austrian hold over northern Italy was consequently shaken. Milan and Venice quickly declared themselves republics. Ferdinando II, Bourbon King of Naples and the Two Sicilies, granted his people a constitution. Europe was in upheaval, and Americans wanted to know the story. So where was Margaret?

In the fall of 1848, Margaret left her baby Angelino with a wet nurse and returned to Rome. Margaret's dispatches for the *Tribune* in 1848-49 are important historical documents. Perry Miller thought them her best writing.

Pius IX was excited to see foreign rule disappearing from Italy but not enthusiastic about the rise of republicanism. The Pope's chief minister was a layman, the cultured, eloquent Count Pellegrino Rossi, but he was widely hated for a simple reason: he was opposed to both reaction and revolution. For him as for his Pope, the road to progress and freedom involved slow reform that maintained continuity and tradition. The followers of Mazzini called Rossi a "tyrant." The leader of the Mazzini radicals was the huge demagogue Angelo Brunetti, better known as Ciceruacchio, the big, fat, filthy Cicero of Pio Nono's Rome. On November 15, 1848 Rossi rode to the Cancelleria, the beautiful High Renaissance building near the Campo dei Fiori where the popular assembly was to meet. As the count stepped out of his coach, Ciceruacchio's son Luigi stabbed him to death. The noisy crowd fell silent. The Papal troops did nothing. Margaret Fuller rejoiced. "For me," she wrote her mother, "I never thought to have heard of a violent death with satisfaction, but this act affected me as one of terrible justice." Garibaldi noted in his diary his pleasure at the death of the "tyrant," then recalled that he was opposed on principle to capital punishment. Such second thoughts, however, were rare among the Mazzinians, who marched through Rome arm in arm, hymning the death of moderation. That evening a crowd marched on the pope's residence, the Quirinal Palace, and in panic the Swiss Guard opened fire. Pius IX wanted to be neither murderer nor victim. On the evening of November 24, 1848, disguised as a simple priest, he fled to Gaeta, which is located on the coast halfway between Rome and Bourbon Naples. Margaret was furious. In her gentler moments, she called Pio Nono weak.

She was also indignant because the American ambassador refused to recognize the newly constituted Roman Republic. If only she were ambassador.... But she was a woman. (In a century, she predicted, things would be different. In fact, in 1952 President Eisenhower appointed Clare Boothe Luce ambassador to Italy. What would Margaret have thought of Luce's play, "The Women"?) Recognition, however, was hardly enough for Margaret Fuller; she wanted the United States to intervene in active support of the Roman Republic. Her radicalization was proceeding apace. She even had a kind word for the Abolitionists, whom she admitted she could not stand when forced to live among them. After the death of Rossi and the flight of the Pope, Mazzini entered Rome in triumph.

Meanwhile, however, the French people voted, by an enormous majority and by universal male suffrage that did not exist in England or the United States, to elect Louis Napoleon their president, and Napoleon had no intention of leaving Rome in the hands of Mazzini and Garibaldi. Soon French troops were approaching the walls of Rome. The trees of Rome were chopped down to prevent sniper fire. Famous villas were destroyed before and during the fighting. Resistance seemed hopeless, but Mazzini wanted Rome martyred, and he got his wish. The city fell in June 1849 for many reasons, among them Garibaldi's insubordination and reckless, though stunning, tactics. Mazzini and Garibaldi went into exile; Pius IX returned. Margaret, Giovanni, and little Angelino fled north to Florence, which Margaret detested. ("It seems like Boston to me.") Impoverished exiles, Margaret, Giovanni, and Angelino decided to sail to America. It was time to tell people about the baby.

The Storys were thunderstruck. How had she kept the secret so long from them? Margaret, who had kept the baby outside of Rome, had told only one close friend of the baby's existence. She had written to her brother Richard but burnt the letter. In one letter to her mother, she had compared herself to Mary Magdalene and asked forgiveness "because she had loved much." The Ossoli family chapel, it should be noted, was in the baroque church of la Maddelena, a short block from the Pantheon.

Amid all the unhappiness, Margaret felt the joys of family life. She was convinced that, with her new family's love to support her, and with the history of the Roman Republic completed, she and her "family" could weather all storms. One storm she did not foresee: just off Fire Island, within sight of New York, a hurricane hit their vessel and sank it with all on board. Margaret, Giovanni, and her manuscript were never found. Only a baby's body, little Angelino, was recovered and found peace, at last, on American soil. Edgar Allan Poe had quipped that the human race was divided into three sexes: men, women, and Margaret Fuller. Italy had turned Margaret into a woman, a mother, and a wife. More or less a wife, at any rate. (One of the mysteries surrounding Margaret Fuller is her marriage. Did she and Giovanni ever tie the knot and if so, when? Evelyn Story says she was shown the marriage certificate, and no one doubts that she thought she saw it.) But Margaret was still, and remains, larger than life.

Her Transcendentalist friends lamented her death, but were nonetheless relieved not to have George Sand in America. They were not ready for that; and, besides, her husband was no de Musset or Chopin. They were sure that he was no nobleman—wrongly. (It is droll to hear Margaret's modern defenders insist that their radical feminist, democrat heroine slept only with a true scion of the Roman nobility.)

Around Margaret hangs always the fascinating aura of the *opus imperfectum.* She wrote *Woman in the Nineteenth Century* before her style had been pruned by writing for Greeley, though the content anticipated contemporary feminism in almost every area, from her insistence that women can hold men's jobs, even be ship captains, to her belief that women's moral sense is distinct from men's. But without question, her best writing is found in her letters and in her articles, both literary and historical, for Greeley's *Tribune.*

Would her history of the Roman Republic have won her the place in American letters she was confident it would? She called her book "a possession forever for man," echoing a famous phrase of Thucydides. In her best literary essay for Greeley, she had discussed American historians, praising Prescott for the readableness of his great histories of the Spanish conquest of America, but she was bothered by his lack of a guiding idea, a void she found filled in Bancroft's work. The people and democracy were her guiding idea, and she had a hero in Mazzini. But did her book possess that impartiality of great histories? Had she left behind the partisan attitude of her newspaper articles? We know from comparing her letters with the articles that Margaret was more critical than the articles would suggest, so perhaps her book would have been an impressive history. But we shall never know for sure.

This is only one of the questions about Margaret Fuller that we cannot answer. There are many others. Would she have raised little Angelino as her father had raised her? Can we trust the partial pictures of her we find in female characters in

Hawthorne's *Blithedale Romance* and *Marble Faun* and Henry James's *Bostonians?* Did she ever feel at home in the world? This last question I think we can answer. In letters from Rome, she often quoted, and always in the same way, a passage from Byron's *Childe Harold's Pilgrimage:* "Oh Rome! my country!" with "my" underlined, against the meter. She knew what she was doing. The orphans of the heart know how to scan their own poetry just as they know their own country, no matter how late in life they come to it, or how little time it is granted them to stay there.

Chapter XIV

PASSION AND PEDANTRY

Lord, what would they say
Did their Catullus walk this way?
—W. B. Yeats

William Butler Yeats's picture of the scholar is not a pretty one ("All cough in ink. All wear the carpet with their shoes."), and literature does not give us many scholarly heroes. Most literary pedants are like George Eliot's Casaubon: boring, impotent in the face of the real world, and, ultimately, not even very good scholars. The rare positive image comes from popular entertainment—Bram Stoker's Van Helsing and Stephen Spielberg's Indiana Jones. Few academics acting as men of letters have any impact outside university circles.

It was different in the last Silver Age of Western civilization, the late nineteenth-century liberal culture that ended with World War I. To take England and the field of classics as an example, it is easy to think of three men with solid scholarly reputations whose names were well known outside the groves of academe: A. E. Housman, Sir James George Frazer, and Gilbert Murray.

Of the three, A. E. Housman's work has stood up best. On either side of the Great War there was a popular frenzy for his poetry, and there still remains a committed group of readers and reciters, some of whom, such as John Sparrow and Christopher Ricks, are distinguished critics. His scholarly writings and critical editions are still important, and his prose is read with pleasure. His early academic career was spotty, however. As an undergraduate at Oxford, Housman won no prizes for Latin verse composition and "was ploughed in Greats," that is, failed his final exams. After taking a pass degree, he won recognition by means of his published works and later became professor of Latin, first at London and then at Cambridge. Although he was a best-selling author and a political conservative, Housman saw his career advance on the basis of its objective merit. Feminists in classics boast that no similar figure could survive today.

The Scottish Sir James G. Frazer, the subject of a recent biography by Robert Ackerman (J. G. Frazer: His Life and Work), won a fellowship at Trinity College, Cambridge, after studying at Glasgow, and it was while holding that fellowship that he made his contributions to scholarship. He spent his career writing long scholarly commentaries on lesser works of classical literature. He interrupted his work on these commentaries, however, to produce in 1890 the two-volume first edition of *The Golden Bough*, which grew to three volumes in the second edition of 1900. The third edition appeared from 1906-1915 in 12 volumes. Both the first and third editions were reprinted as late as the 1970s, and his one-volume abridgment of 1922 was a best-seller. Frazer's combination of 18th-century pomposity and immense learning won him fame that reached popular adulation. Stanley Edgar Hyman's *The Tangled Bank* (1956) ranks Frazer with Darwin, Marx, and Freud for his influence on the modern world. In recent decades, some of the most creative scholars in the humanities are still citing and discussing Frazer, as one can see in René Girard's study of the scapegoat and Walter Burkert's work on ritual in Greek tragedy and mythology. (Robert Ackerman knows nothing of Frazer's significance but instead tells us that "Not only are his answers superseded, but more important his questions likewise are no longer relevant.") Despite his considerable scholarly achievements, Frazer received no academic honor from Cambridge other than his Trinity College fellowship. (After World War I friends established with private funds the Frazer Lectureship at Cambridge, but, on the whole, Cambridge ignored him.) Frazer did win a professorship at Liverpool at one point, honorary degrees from Oxford and the Sorbonne, and a knighthood.

Gilbert Murray—a recent book by Sir Duncan Wilson called *Gilbert Murray, O.M. 1866-1957* is worth reading—had, of the three men, the most spectacular academic career. He won prize after prize at his public school and at Oxford, and directly out of university (1889), Murray was appointed to the chair of Greek at Glasgow because of his marvelous ability to compose Greek prose. He resigned after ten years, but in 1908 Oxford appointed him Regius Professor of Greek, a chair he held until 1936. His translations of Euripides were the standard English versions for the first half of the century. Before World War I he was a major figure in the theatrical cult of "Ibsenity." The figure of Adolphus Cusins in Shaw's *Major Barbara* is modeled on Murray. (Murray's wife and mother-in-law appear as, respectively, Barbara and Barbara's mother. Shaw jokingly called the play "Murray's Mother-in-Law.") His scholarly writing before the Great War was of international significance. After the war Murray headed the League of Nations Union, and his books and talks on the BBC continued to appear until his death.

The contemporary reader may well ask why three such creative, public figures had chosen early on to become what Robert Ackerman calls "professional students of that least practical of subjects, classics." But as Ackerman's own survey of the Cambridge examination system shows, knowledge of Greek and Latin was essential for anyone in nineteenth-century England interested in an academic or religious career—or in being a highly visible arbiter of culture, which Housman, Frazer, and Murray became. (Greek, for instance, was a prerequisite for study at Oxford until 1920.) The Brits knew what they were doing in having these requirements. Serious research in the humanities, as well as creative work in them, is impossible without a good knowledge of Greek and Latin—as I once heard René Girard tell a group of horror-struck students of comparative literature. Lacking a classical education, a Frazer or a Housman today could never accomplish what those men did. By studying the classics, and thus having access to the whole humane tradition of the West, Housman, Frazer, and Murray had something cogent and interesting to say to men of their generation, and the public, as well as their pupils, listened.

All three men suffered from a common Victorian malady. They had lost their faith in orthodox Christianity. Housman, the conservative, did not force his view on others. He even wrote a hymn to be sung at his own funeral. Frazer, on the contrary, early saw a mission to disabuse the world of superstition. *The Golden Bough*, in all three complete editions, is a barely disguised polemic against Christianity. In his obituary of his best friend, the great Semiticist Robertson Smith, Frazer explained that the study of comparative religions "proves that many religious doctrines and practices are based on primitive conceptions which most civilized and educated men have long agreed in abandoning as mistaken. From this it is a natural and often a probable inference that doctrines so based are false, and that practices so based are foolish." Ackerman expresses amazement that Frazer would use the death of his best friend as an excuse for religious polemic, especially since this view of the comparative method was not that of the deceased man himself. Frazer, however, was a man obsessed. Frazer even attempted in the second edition of *The Golden Bough* to prove that the passion of Jesus was a misinterpretation by early Christians of a Passover ritual. It was one of his most catastrophic scholarly hypotheses. After this hypothesis was thoroughly refuted even to his satisfaction, Frazer reprinted the passion story in the third edition but as an example of the kind of thing that *might* have happened. Frazer's revolt against his Scottish evangelical background would not let go of him. He could not help himself. His wife talked him out of including the story in the 1922 one-volume abridgment, but thankfully Robert Fraser has included it in his "new abridgement" published by Oxford in 1994.

The same anti-Christian motif winds through the popular and scholarly writings of Gilbert Murray. Even his major scholarly work, *The Rise of the Greek Epic,* has as a minor chord an attack on Christian scriptures. Murray's appointment to the Regius chair kept him from delivering the prestigious Gifford Lectures on religion, but we know that he intended to explain, had he been given the chance, his "profound belief in ethics and disbelief in all revelational religions." As late as 1940 he was reprinting his World War I attacks on Christianity and defense of paganism, especially Stoicism.

Frazer and Murray were important forces for convincing educated people that ethics and progress could survive without the accidental historical garb of Christianity. Then came the Great War and its aftermath, and Frazer and Murray, along with the rest of liberal Europe, had a chance to see how long-lasting and influential ethics were now that the religious foundations of morality had been undermined. The effects of mechanistic, Enlightenment thinking in the war to end all wars were evident: England and France's cynical alliance with the brutal Russian state against Germany, Germany's reckless invasion of Belgium, the use of poison gas by both sides. The collapse of prewar liberal dreams in the wake of this savage behavior hit home, slowly but surely, on the liberal psyche. Housman, however, had never been fooled. As early as 1900 he had written to Murray, who was later to write British war propaganda, "I rather doubt if man really has much to gain by substituting peace for strife, as you and Jesus Christ recommend."

By 1933 Frazer had finally realized what was happening, and he spoke out in an essay on the hero of his youth, Condorcet: "The words of fiery eloquence in which Edmund Burke, the wisest of political thinkers, branded the Jacobins of his day are applicable, with hardly a change but that of names, to the Bolsheviks of our day. In Russia of today, as in France of the day before yesterday, we see the same systematic and determined attacks on those institutions which hitherto have been regarded as the very pillars of civilised society; I mean the institutions of private property, the family, and religion." Religion, which was false doctrine and foolish practice in 1894, was now a pillar of civilized society. In his obituary of Robertson Smith, Frazer had predicted that insofar as our ethics rest on religious or theological foundations, the unsettling of those foundations would "call for a reconsideration of the speculative basis of ethics." He had not then thought through the practical ramifications of this reconsideration.

Murray changed, too. When Anthony Eden attacked Egypt in 1956 in defense of the Suez canal, Murray spoke out in measured approbation. Near the end of his life he wrote his son-in-law, Arnold Toynbee, "I get the horrors when I think of enormous numbers of Russians, Chinese, and possibly Arabs and of coloured people—a vast sea of barbarism round an island of Hellenism.... I begin to think that we should aim not at a peaceful law-abiding world, but at some form of unity of Christian or Hellenic civilisation."

The future seemed so bright in the days before the Great War. We at the end of the twentieth century cannot imagine the optimism at the century's inception, when Housman, Frazer, and Murray were in their prime. The force of liberal public opinion, in Yeats's words, made "old wrong melt down, as if it were wax in the sun's rays." "O but we dreamed to mend whatever mischief seemed to afflict mankind"—superstition, hard liquor, and the German emperor. If people would only turn away from revelational religion and devote themselves to ethics and science, the world would soon be perfect. Yeats, however, saw things differently. "We fed the heart on fantasies," he wrote. "The heart's grown brutal from the fare." Housman, too, was skeptical about the future, but even he never dreamed what nightmares were in store for a Europe that so easily gave up its Christian heritage. Gilbert Murray and J. G. Frazer were completely caught by surprise.

So is there a lesson to be learned from the examples of these three? If Housman, Frazer, and Murray, classicists all, failed to see the terror coming, of what use are volume after volume of classical studies? One answer might be that classicists need a greater appreciation for Christianity's role in saving the classics. As Etienne Gilson wrote in his *History of Christian Philosophy in the Middle Ages*, "In point of fact, it is not philosophy that kept Christianity alive during fourteen centuries, rather, it is Christianity that did not allow philosophy to perish." The same may be said of all classical culture, not just philosophy. A second answer is that all men, regardless of education—even thoroughly classical education—must be, at least in part, men of their time, and like most people in England at the time, Housman, Frazer, and Murray did not appreciate just how late in the day it was for liberal England. In the end, they deserve better than a comparison to George Eliot's Casaubon, because each had the courage to repent, in a sense, from the erroneous belief in progress when its promises proved vain. It takes character to reverse the opinions of a lifetime, even with evidence like World War I and the Russian Revolution in front of you. Today we look around in vain for men like those three classicists of late liberal England, A. E. Housman, Sir James Frazer, and Gilbert Murray, O.M.

Chapter XV

J. R. R. TOLKIEN:
INVENTING LOST WORLDS

The American tourists were visiting Rome for the first time and asked the owner of their *pensione* what to see. He urged them not to miss the Roman Forum. When they returned for lunch, they were quiet and grim mouthed. Finally, he asked them why, and the man burst out, "We never dreamed that you Italians were such chauvinists. We ask a polite question in good faith and you send us to some place we bombed during the war."

It is sometimes hard for the reader of the daily newspapers to remember that there are ruins not created by the 20th century. Among the ancient wrecks tourists visit is the *doctus poeta*, as the Romans called him, the scholar-poet; unlike the ruins he haunted, however, he really is a victim of this century. Virgil, Dante, Milton, and Tasso have no successors as the twentieth century draws to a close. Today's universities may provide refuge for a few poets and token "creative writers," but in general the university in the West cannot comprehend, let alone foster, the humane ideal of the *doctus poeta.*

Scholar-poets have indeed existed in this century, but they have been largely misunderstood. A. E. Housman is a good example. Recent years have seen several well-received biographies, each of which concentrates on the few months of his writing poetry and his pitiable love life. Housman's many volumes of scholarly work, which rescued English classical studies from provincialism and mediocrity, are viewed as a *parergon*, something to fill in the years. The tone was set by Edmund Wilson, who sneered at Housman's scholarship; you see, Housman edited the Silver Latin poets, Juvenal and Lucan, and refused to publish his edition of the Augustan love poet, Propertius. What Wilson did not understand is the centrality of Juvenal the Satirist for modern culture and the importance of Lucan and Roman *libertas* for contemporary freedom.

Wilson also had his innings at J. R. R. Tolkien, another of this century's scholar-poets. Wilson the literary critic read in the publisher's press release that the professor of English and former professor of Anglo-Saxon had located the origins of *The Lord of the Rings* in his "secret vice" of inventing languages—languages which then needed a mythology and history in which to grow and develop like historical languages. Wilson was aghast. A narrative that grew from a desire to root an invented language in story and folklore—how could the tale ever be more than "a philological curiosity."

We do soon tire of the complicated narrative and highfalutin language used in the stories that lie behind *The Lord of the Rings* and long for the company of Frodo and Sam Gamgee. It is as if we had picked up a book in our motel room, expecting to enjoy the vigorous dialogue of St. John's Gospel, only to find ourselves wandering with the children of Nephi through the Book of Mormon. But say not the labour naught availeth. *The Lost Tales* and *The Silmarillion* gave to *The Lord of the Rings* its depth of concreteness in language and history. Similarly, without the pedantry and sometimes misconceived ingenuity that we find in his lectures on the Old English Exodus and the Finn Fragment, Tolkien could not have rendered *Beowulf* alive and renewed.

To give us a taste of Tolkien's two philologies, the fantastical and the historical, Christopher Tolkien has edited several of his father's lectures as *The Monsters and the Critics and Other Essays*. Relevance to *The Lord of the Rings* was the criterion for including the essays "A Secret Vice," "On Fairy-Stories," and even "English and Welsh," since Welsh was used as a model for some of the names in the *Rings* trilogy. The title essay, "*Beowulf*: The Monsters and the Critics," which was first a lecture given in 1936 and later published in 1937, may also have been included on this criterion. In the piece Tolkien explains how a Christian writer could create a fictional world true to the drama of Christian morality without mentioning

Christ—which is what Tolkien did in writing the *Rings*.

"*Beowulf*: The Monsters and the Critics" deals mainly with *Beowulf*. It is hardly saying too much to say that this one essay changed forever the study of a major work in the canon of English literature. It rescued *Beowulf* from its status as a "philological curiosity" and established it as a major literary work.

To appreciate the importance of "The Monsters and the Critics" one must first work slowly through *Beowulf*, preferably in Friedrich Klaeber's great edition (1928), which is still in print after more than 70 years, one of the greatest works of scholarship to emerge from the American university system. Notwithstanding all of Klaeber's indispensable apparatus for understanding the poem's roots in etymology and comparative folklore, Klaeber discusses the poem's narrative structure only once, in a famous paragraph on its "lack of steady advance." How much more efficiently Icelandic sagas killed their monsters than their Old English counterparts! Later criticism of the poem (like R. W. Chambers' *Beowulf: An Introduction*) concentrated almost exclusively on historical, rather than on literary, questions. Given the history of the commentary on the poem, it is not surprising that in 1936 Tolkien wrote that "*Beowulf* has been used as a quarry of fact and fancy far more assiduously than it has been studied as a work of art."

"The Monsters and the Critics" redresses the balance. It touches on most of the poem's problems, from the putative

influence of Latin epic, through its vision of the German heroic ideal, to the mind, at once Christian and elegiac, that created *Beowulf*. To call *Beowulf* studies since 1936 a series of footnotes to Tolkien would be unjust—and yet how often even the
most original work ends up reflecting or rejecting Tolkien's
apodictic insights. For example, *Beowulf: The Poem and Its Tradition* by Berkeley's John D. Niles is a thorough and thought-
provoking study, with chapters on areas that scarcely existed in
1936. But despite its originality and critical insight, Niles's book
serves to confirm Tolkien's thesis (or only slightly modifies it).
Following a generation that made St. Augustine more central
for understanding the poem than the German heroic ideal, Niles
returns to Tolkien's belief that *Beowulf* is a poem by a Christian
poet, but not a Christian poem.

Despite his ability to illuminate *Beowulf* as a literary work,
Tolkien never saw himself as a literary critic. His "Valedictory
Address" is quite clear about his scholarly origins in the "language," or philological, side of the split in the Oxford English
faculty. But he did have the literary critical gift. To the extent
Tolkien's assessment of himself in this address is correct, however, the essays in *The Monsters and the Critics* are misleading about
Tolkien's true contributions to scholarship and teaching. More
representative of his work are his text, commentary, and translation of *The Old English Exodus* (edited by Joan Turville-Petre),
and *Finn and Hengest: The Fragment and the Episode* (edited by Alan

Bliss). In the latter, Tolkien takes a brief and fragmentary tale sung by a bard in *Beowulf* and a fragment of a separate version of the same story that survives on a single manuscript page and tries to reconstruct the history that lies behind the two sources. Not surprisingly, Tolkien sees it as the story of the fall of a great, prehistoric people and the birth of a new age. The Jutes fall with the death of their young prince, but Hengest rises from the tragedy to lead the German people into Celtic Britain and found Anglo-Saxon England. We are moved by the scope and sympathy of the reconstruction even while acknowledging that too little of the original text survives for certainty, and that some aspects of the argument are forced or unlikely.

Tolkien's philological reconstruction of the *Beowulf* fragments reminds us of what he said about that great epic and the *Aeneid:* "The real resemblance of the *Aeneid* and *Beowulf* lies in the constant presence of a sense of many-storied antiquity." It is a trait both works share with *The Lord of the Rings.* With *Beowulf* too much is lost for a secure reconstruction of its mythological or historical backdrop. Much more can be done for the *Aeneid,* and a great deal for *The Lord of the Rings.* Behind its hints of ages and great races almost vanished from memory lies a detailed history, composed, of course, by Tolkien himself. (Christopher Tolkien published part of that history as *The Silmarillion* [1977] before editing the original versions of those stories as *The Book of Lost Tales: Part One* and *Part Two* [both 1984 in America]. The characters and themes of the *Lost Tales* are closely related to *The Silmarillion*, but there are many differences: "Beren is an Elf, not a Man, and his captor, the ultimate precursor of Sauron in that role, is a monstrous cat inhabited by a fiend; the Dwarves are an evil people; and the historical relations of Quenya and Sindarin [the Elvish tongues] were quite differently conceived.")

In his clever essay "On Fairy-Stories," Tolkien defended the aesthetic—and Christian—rightness of the eucatastrophic closure, the Happy Ending. Herein may lie the true difference between philologist and literary critic. The literary critic is a perpetual optimist. He sees a work attacked or misunderstood, waves his magic pen, and *voilà*, all is light. Like some doctors, he tends to ignore or even blame the fragmentary and broken that he cannot restore to wholeness. The philologist, however, lives in the tragic world of the partially lost or broken. He knows that an 18th-century fire ate away exactly that page of *Beowulf* that explains why the dragon attacks after so many ages of rest. He knows of an entire language, Gothic, which is lost except for one translation of the Gospels. Yet he maintains a hope, not born of optimism (he will never recover that piece) but of gratitude. "We have," he says to himself, "so much of the story even so. How wonderful it is." The missing makes the remaining precious. The classical philologist Housman tried to rescue from scattered medieval manuscripts, and in the face of his century's false scientific method and falser romantic sensibility, what has survived of Latin poetry—and his work still inspires a continuing rescue operation, which is at least as vital to the world of letters as his few score gloomy lyrics. Tolkien performed the same function for his field of ancient Northern languages and myths.

Tolkien, who in his youth had worked on the *Oxford English Dictionary*, knew that, once upon a time, "grammar" and "glamour" were the same word, and he devoted his life as pedant and poet to helping us feel that unity as a living reality. "Man is in love," said Yeats, "and loves what vanishes. What more is there to say?" Both literary critic and philologist have much more to say, of course. But while the literary critic is using his rational mind to create the best of all possible literary worlds, *Beowulf* fights the eerie dragon of destruction, the devourer of languages, of manuscripts, of human memory. And the philologist fights with him. "You and I," Professor Tolkien wrote his son, "belong to the ever-defeated, never altogether subdued side." He stands next to the old Norse gods, of whom he liked to quote W. P. Ker: "They are on the right side, though it is not the side that wins. The winning side is Chaos and Unreason, but the gods, who are defeated, think that defeat no refutation."

Section III

Contemporary Chronicles: Role Models and Popular Culture

Chapter XVI

RUSSELL KIRK: BOHEMIAN TORY

Russell Kirk once called the South "The Permanence of the American nation." He went there after the Second World War to seek a master of arts degree among the ersatz traditional loveliness of Duke University and had came to know a part of America (as he put it in *Confessions of a Bohemian Tory*) "which had captured my imagination years before, in books...: Richmond and Charleston and Savannah, cities that had not surrendered incontinent to the new order of American life: and quiet corners like Petersburg, in Virginia, and Hillsborough, in North Carolina, and Fernandina Island, in Florida." It was in this environment that he "first began to apprehend" the ideas and insights of Edmund Burke—in a land where it still made sense to talk of "prescriptive rights," "the unbought grace of life," "the spirit of religion and the spirit of a gentleman."

Kirk himself had claim to the title "Permanence of American

Conservatism." Mr. Buckley once observed that he could never be sure what it meant to be a conservative, but that he could spot a liberal across a crowded room. Russell Kirk, however, could spot conservatism in some interesting places. He spotted a conservative element, for instance, in the Jeffersonian Randolph of Roanoke, the subject of his M.A. thesis at Duke, and in Ray Bradbury, the master of science fiction. He could also detect the Manchester smog hovering over an "individualist" or the populist lurking in Willmoore Kendall, the distinguished scholar for whom the Federalist Papers were "the Laws of the Medes and Persians which change not."

Russell Kirk was the object of considerable polemic in his lifetime. Morton Auerbach wrote *The Conservative Illusion* (1959) to refute Kirk's "philosophy" (along with Plato's and a few other people's). Willmoore Kendall had planned a book, *The Sages of Conservatism*, to show that Kirk and every other prominent conservative intellectual of the 1950s and 60s were pseudo-sages leading conservatism down the wrong path. But Kirk was never a metaphysician or a ward-heeler, let alone a pseudo-sage. If I had to provide a job description for affirmative action, I suppose I would call Kirk a man of letters, which was his term for himself. His "work" fits into that grey area where the scholar fades into the journalist, that in-between place having appeal to high-and middlebrow readers alike. More important than Kirk's job, however, was his vocation:

to be an *exemplum* of genuine conservatism.

Kirk presented America with an attitude, a style, a persona. Born in a disintegrating little town in Michigan, a student at the barren Michigan State University during the Depression (when a scholarship provided escape from unemployment), rootless, unmarried, and wandering for much of his early life—from graduate school, to the Ford Company's Rouge plant, to a stint in the Army in the Great Salt Lake Desert, back as a professor to Michigan State University, which he soon left in a pique—Kirk was a Bohemian Tory. He once said of himself, "I do not happen to be a Catholic, or an Anglican, or a disciple of Dr. Niebuhr.... I am an archaic Puritan, which is much the same thing as a Gothic Jew.... Unlike my mentor, Dr. Samuel Johnson, heterodoxy is my doxy, not orthodoxy." It was out of a spirit of contradiction that he suggested to a surprised group of colleagues that "the fear of God is the beginning of wisdom." He discovered that the most efficient way for an *enfant terrible* to *épater les intelligentsia* in our day is to repeat (if I may quote Senator McCarthy out of context) "the most unheard of things they ever heard of," the truths men keep coming back and back to.

"What are you and I?" Kirk asked. "In large part we are what we imagine ourselves to be. William Butler Yeats advises us to clap masks to our faces and play our appropriate part: the image becomes reality. There is something, after all, in

Randolph's bold admonition: 'Make unto yourselves an image, and, in defiance of the Decalogue, worship it.'" The young Kirk had found his mask in conservatism.

Kirk became a contemporary incarnation of Max Beerbohm's Happy Hypocrite. Kirk set out to play the orotund Sage of Traditionalism: living in an old house, christened Piety Hill, in his home town of Mecosta and typing his books and articles and stories "on my great-uncle Raymond's typewriter, an L. C. Smith No. 1, circa 1907; perhaps my heir will use it after me." And what happened to Lord Harry Hell happened to him. One day a lovely woman took off his mask and found beneath it a living face that matched. Kirk lived rooted at Piety Hill; he married and had children; he was visited by young conservatives; and he even became a Catholic—so he could finally say with Johnson, "orthodoxy is my doxy." Like Horace, like Yeats, Kirk became his own most resonant symbol of the possibility of meaningful conservatism in a personal existence.

After he put on his mask, Russell Kirk began spouting not his own words, but other people's. Indeed, quotation, from Burke and the Burkean tradition, which he has done so much to define, forms the most striking trait of Kirk's style. No topic, no book, no personality can appear before this Burkean Linnaeus and escape the tag of the appropriate citation. Clinton Rossiter once described Kirk as one of those "who have belaboured liberalism in season and out." (Willmoore Kendall asked, "What

months of the year, one wonders, has Rossiter set aside as the
'season' for 'belabouring' liberals?") What Russell Kirk did do
"in season and out" was not merely to scourge liberals but to
discuss the issues of the day either in a language derived from
the Burkean tradition, or by means of quoted passages from
Burke himself. Rossiter wrote in both editions of *Conservatism
in America* that Kirk "has the sound of a man born one hundred and fifty years too late and in the wrong country." Few of
Kirk's pages, however, replete as they are with quotation after
Burkean quotation, are less relevant than when Kirk composed
them. I wonder whether the same can be said of Rossiter's works.
Kirk reviewed the issues and figures of the day in a vocabulary
and with a pace and rhythm that, because of its spaciousness,
permitted reflection while reading. Kirk's English, which could
be mulled over while being read, was quite an achievement in
our journalistic day.

Russell Kirk often pictured himself as the voice of one crying in the wilderness, with only the rarest of reassuring signals
from the Remnant. In no area was he so justified as education.
America's problems in this field were analyzed clearly and co-
gently by Kirk and others more than a generation ago. In all
that time little has been done to avert a national catastrophe of
illiteracy in a country dependent on formal education for an
informed electorate and a cultural elite, as well as for a technology that needs constantly to renew itself or die.

Kirk's criticisms of education stretch over a generation and more, back to an article in the *South Atlantic Quarterly* for 1945. A moralist, who trusted small schools and the commitment of teacher and student, he was already dubious in 1954 of Buckley's appeal to committed *alumni*, and in 1978 he confessed himself "no enthusiast" for the Great Books curriculum, though he spoke favorably of those who had passed through it. (It is surprising, given his devotion to the ideals of Newman, that Kirk did not devote more effort to urging church involvement in education, though there are good pages on this in *The Intemperate Professor*.) In his *Theory of Education in the United States*, given first as lectures in 1931 at the University of Virginia, Albert J. Nock said that what we need are not machines, devices, buildings, programs, but insight into the *raison d'être* of education. Without that, no reform will avail; our educational system will never be able to remodel itself into an effective instrument, because we shall have either no model or at best a false one (of professionalism, most likely). Kirk would have agreed.

From the first, Kirk saw the origin of the abandonment of standards in education, now widely acknowledged, in the draining of religion from American education. The religious element jettisoned, the commitment to the individual soul suffered neglect, and so the race for higher enrollments and lower standards was on, with the cheerleaders prancing to the cries of "democracy" and "greater opportunity for all."

Kirk's political attitude, which reflected the reactionary fires that had burned in fierce opposition to the French Revolution, must have sounded "one hundred and fifty years too late and in the wrong country" to a 1950s America basking in postwar prosperity with the Republican Party safely under the thumb of Dwight Eisenhower. It was a time when moderate liberals like Rossiter and Peter Viereck called themselves "conservatives" and were believed. A similar situation in the 1920s provoked T. S. Eliot to write in the "Preface" to *For Lancelot Andrewes* (1928) of "what is almost worse than clap-trap, I mean temperate conservatism." In the 1960s, however, the Gods of the Copybook Headings (one of Kirk's favorite phrases) returned with a vengeance on the heads of sweetness-and-light liberals. Conservatives, brought up on a political philosophy that had already confronted the revolution in France two hundred years earlier, were prepared, intellectually and emotionally. As A. E. Housman put it,

> The thoughts of others
>> Were light and fleeting,
>> Of lovers' meeting
> Of luck or fame.
> Mine were of trouble,
>> And mine were steady;
>> So I was ready
> When trouble came.

The trendy Liberal was not ready and all too often was left to face surrender, disgrace, and, in poor Rossiter's case, despair—the sickness unto death.

The continuing vitality of Burke's insights forms the *leitmotif* of Kirk's many books of intellectual history: *The Conservative Mind*; his book on Randolph of Roanoke (1951); his study of Senator Robert Taft (1967); his literary criticism of T. S. Eliot (1971); and his biography of Burke himself (1967). The quotations from Burke and the parallelisms of situation in these works are far from window dressing. These devices are the essence of these books and make them worth reading.

Can Burke really be the basis for an intellectually radical conservatism? Must not a Burkean, like Peter Viereck, dedicate himself to the defense of our Great and Glorious Revolution of 1933, a revolution not made but prevented by Tory democrat FDR? Are not New Deal Democrats the real conservatives of the institutions and traditions of our land as it really is? John Crowe Ransom, in a notably negative review of *The Conservative Mind*, saw the conservatives' role as that of "a brake against alteration;" of opposing innovation but only modifying its extremes, and then defending the new old once it is established, along with the old old. Kirk "is still saying Burke, but actually he wants the conservatives to appropriate the very reforms against which they have fought and advance them under the party colors.... The conservative mind is not unable, as has been charged, to learn any lesson from the changes of history. It is only unable to recite the lesson faithfully."

In defense of Kirk, however, it must be said that, like everyone else, conservative, liberal, and radical, Kirk distinguished among trends he wanted continued, beleaguered realities he wanted defended, and lost beauties he wanted restored. John Crowe Ransom was no different in his own writings. Kirk did tend over time to talk less of prescriptive rights and more of "the Permanent Things" (T. S. Eliot), "norms," "the spirit of religion and the spirit of a gentleman." It is true that the principles we act on and judge by are indeed rooted, finally, in a reality beyond our experience and so determined by God. But this reality is revealed to us most often in certain historical, limited circumstances; our principles are encrusted or protected by other, lesser realities that one removes at the peril of sapping the emotive and imaginative core that makes truth speak to the individual heart. Ultimately, nothing can shake the divinely rooted nature of reality, but Kirk was sensitive to the history-bound reality through which we perceive and are touched by capital "T" truths. The ancient Rabbis referred to "building a wall around the Law." A traditionalist sees himself as defending, not building, these historical growths, but in truth he does both. Atheist conservatives prefer the tried and true over the untested. Even liberals speak of Future Shock these days.

Kirk examined this dual heritage, the divinely rooted and the historically grounded, in *The Roots of American Order* (1971), which was written as a high school textbook, "as directly and simply as was in me." Both the range of topics and the vocabulary are beyond high school and even college students, but the work is interesting as a variation on Kirk's usual method. We see him searching out what our Founding Fathers valued in the civilization of the ancient, medieval, and modern worlds. It is not *The Conservative Mind from Moses to Burke.* Kirk often said that it makes no sense to talk of conservatism before Burke, and his statement near the end of *The Conservative Mind* that "the immediate political connections of Sophocles, Virgil, and Dante were those which, by rough analogy, we now call 'conservative'" does not contradict that opinion. Kirk examines the discoveries made in and through history of certain political and religious truths and how those discoveries survived to influence, to inform, and to create America. The Permanent Things are, as their name suggests, what has persisted down the centuries to us, rooted in history and God's will.

"Yet cheerfulness keeps breaking in" (another of Russell Kirk's favorite phrases). America now sees itself as conservative. The adherents of "disintegrated Liberalism" still cling to their strongholds, especially in the Academy and government, but they debate with a sad weariness, like religious conservatives at the end of the last century. More and more people see in the horror of liberalism's last drunken binge what they want to avoid for themselves and their children. Much has been lost or destroyed, yet much remains. Among that "much" stood the figure of Russell Kirk, defender, interpreter, *exemplum virtutis.* Armed with the Roman senator's *libertas* as well as his *gravitas,* he was not afraid to criticize or praise outside the boundaries of approved opinion, finding nuggets of truth in Sidney Hook and George Gissing, or *errata et corrigenda* in Frank Meyer and William Buckley. But Russell Kirk is more than the sum of his writings. He is the scout pointing the way to the land of heart's content, which could be the Past, or the permanence of the South, but can also be little Mecosta, Michigan. He is the friend who has introduced us to departed comrades who enrich our lives.

Russell Kirk understood that our lives are not monologues, written and performed by stand-up comics, alone in a spotlight. "All the world's a stage," as Shakespeare saw, and we all have our parts to act and our lines to read. Only an exceptional few, however, write their own lines. Once upon a time a good many people knew what they needed to say when the time came: from the Bible, the Greek and Latin classics, or the great works of their own national literatures. That situation has passed. Faced with a moment of high decision, or great joy or tragedy, the average person is mute or confused. Until the day he died, Russell Kirk faithfully stood by, repeating for those who cared to listen the words we all need to know. He rarely raised his voice, but he never swerved from his mission. For that, those who listened and remembered will always be grateful.

Chapter XVII

DOUGLAS YOUNG:
A FREE-MINDED SCOT

Douglas Young was a tall man, six feet six inches; with his beard he looked like a Calvinist Jehovah. At St. Andrews, he acquired the nickname "God." A group was discussing the violent situation in the Balkans and was stumped over the identity of a political leader in the region. (Even in the 1930s, the Balkans were full of angry ethnic factions fighting and killing one another.) "God alone knows his name," one of them muttered. "Well, I know his name," said Douglas, "and I shall tell it to you." For a game of charades at Oxford, he was carried in upside down as a clue for the word "dog." (The editors of his memorial volume, A Clear Voice, call this a legend, but Nigel Nicolson in My Oxford, My Cambridge says he helped carry Douglas in.)

Douglas' father, an officer in the Bengal Artillery, was a Tory and an Imperialist, but, apart from politics, a loyal Scot.

Douglas was a Unionist until 1929, when he was at Merchiston Castle School in Edinburgh. The poet Lewis Spence's campaign for Parliament as a Scots Nationalist appealed to Douglas' natural conservatism and made him "an assertor of my own country's right to self-government." He went to St. Andrews, despite passing the entrance exams for Oxford and Cambridge, and read the great Gaelic poet Sorley MacLean (Somhairle MacGill-Eain) and the Scots poet Hugh MacDiarmid (né C. M. Grieve). Although president of the Conservative Club, he worked in 1933 for Scots Nationalist Eric Linklater's candidacy for Parliament.

Douglas loved ancient Greek and was very good at it. For a career in classics, however, he had to study at Cambridge or Oxford. He chose the latter and spent four years at New College. ("We were New College because slightly later in the fourteenth century than William of Wykeham's other establishment, Winchester School.") He was president of the Scottish Society and advocated giving social democracy a fair trial. (Unlike his friends MacLean and MacDiarmid, he was never a Communist. In his 1943 speech "William Wallace and This War," he referred contemptuously to "the now popular Mr. Djugashvili, alias Stalin.") He earned the friendship of older, more traditional scholars, like W. M. Lindsay of St. Andrews and T. W. Allen at Oxford, but not the leaders of the next generation. On C. M. Bowra, the "Great Teacher" of his time, he wrote the best limerick ever composed in ancient Greek. Eduard Fraenkel, the Corpus Professor of Latin and a refugee from Hitler's Germany, conceived a profound dislike for Douglas. In his final translation examinations from English into Greek and Latin, Douglas wrote, not two, but all four compositions in Greek and Latin poetry and prose. Fraenkel accused him of cheating, because no one could do it. The scholar Fraenkel most admired at Oxford, Sir John Beasley, the founder of the study of Greek vase painting, blandly assured Fraenkel that it could be done. "You see, I did it." (As an undergraduate, Beasley had composed a famous parody in Ionic Greek of Herodotus' visit to England, "Herodotus at the Zoo.")

In 1938, Douglas turned down Oxford's prestigious Craven fellowship to teach at Aberdeen and joined the Scottish Nationalist Party (SNP). War was coming, and the SNP's official position was that its members were not to serve in the British military until Scotland had been granted dominion status, with its own parliament, like Canada or New Zealand.

As with the Balkans, Scotland's story for independence goes back a long way. When Queen Elizabeth died in 1603, the crown devolved upon the head of the son of her old *bête noire*, Mary Queen of Scots. James VI of Scotland, who was James I of England as well, made a fateful decision. He transferred the royal court to London. The King James Bible was

translated, as a result, into English, instead of Scots, and
Scotland's affairs were put on the back burner. The next century was chaotic and violent for both nations. By 1707, England was again ruled by a childless old woman, Anne. At her
death the throne was to be handed over to the Elector of
Hanover and his line, so the relationship of the two kingdoms
of England and Scotland had to be regularized. By the Treaty
of Union of 1707 these two countries became Great Britain,
and their parliaments were amalgamated into the British Parliament. In practice, it was the old English Parliament with a
rump minority of 45 Scottish members (71 in Douglas' day)
with 16 Scots in the House of Lords, who were regularly out-
voted or ignored. Attempts to restore the rightful heir to the
Scottish throne were ruthlessly put down by the British crown
in 1715 and 1745. From that time on England ruled Scotland as a conquered province. England did grant all rights and
duties of British citizenship to any Scot who moved to England, but many emigrated overseas, where Scots excelled in
many fields. Douglas estimated at some 20 million the Scottish Diaspora throughout the English-speaking world, *Scotti per
diversa vagantes.*

Taking the story down to the twentieth century: Douglas
felt that during the Kaiser's War, Scottish troops had suffered
disproportionately heavy losses by being placed by the English
at greater risk than English troops. Scotland's economy had

suffered more than England's from the wartime state socialism as well as from the postwar slump, since, to quote Douglas, English "governments, though stupid, were at least primarily concerned with England." The SNP correctly predicted similar policies in the next war (though they did not foresee that the British government would set up most new factories for war *matériel* in England and draft Scottish women to labor in the distant and dangerous English industrial cities).

At a May Day (Labor Day) rally in Aberdeen in 1939, as war loomed, a heckler asked Douglas whether the Treaty of Union gave the British Parliament the authority to draft Scotsmen for foreign service. Douglas gave the official SNP position, that Article XVIII of the Treaty of Union preserved the Scottish Common Law and, so drafting Scots was *ultra vires*, beyond the authority, of the British Parliament. The crowd cheered.

Douglas was in Greece when Hitler invaded Poland on September 1, 1939. Conscription was enacted. The SNP split into pacifists, anti-Nazis, and stand patters. (The communists were silent. Russia was an ally of Nazi Germany.) Douglas stood his ground: "Dominion self-government in war as in peace, and no acquiescence in the unconstitutional conscription, either for military purposes or, as was soon imposed, for industrial work," as he wrote in his postwar memoir, *Chasing an Ancient Greek*.

The initial round of conscription had passed Douglas by,

but the terrible early defeats soon led to men in their late 20s being "dereserved." Douglas might have been able to avoid service because of his height, poor eyesight, and the effects of a childhood injury. Nonetheless, he refused to answer his draft notice and was summoned to the local Sheriff-Court to answer charges.

On April 13, 1942, Douglas appeared before Sheriff Norman MacDonald in Glasgow. Repudiating the name "British," he asserted that "no government other than a Scottish government has any rights over the Scots." He doubted British competence. "I observe the British government conducting its so-called war effort with such fusionless incompetence as to give a walkover to the imperialist ventures of the Germans, the Americans, and the Japanese." Given the way Churchill was running it, he felt the war would end with the loss of the British Empire and with world hegemony handed over either to the Axis or America. (Was he wrong?) "To judge by recent results," he continued, "there is great doubt about the capacity of the British government to defend Scotland, which is my country. It is no service to Scotland to follow the misleadership of the British government and become a prisoner at St. Valery-en-Caux or at Singapore or elsewhere."

Scotland was one of the sovereign nations of Europe, according to Douglas, not an English province. "Scots troops have played the part of Uriah the Hittite often enough already in

Great Britain's wars, and it is now high time the Scots decided to fight for Scots independence, following the example of the Serbs, the Norse, and other self-respecting nations." Serbia and Norway had both been invaded by Nazi Germany. The comparison was a provocation. "Scots workers, women as well as men, are transported like coolies to labor for an alien imperialism furth of Scotland, while Scotland is invaded by a swarm of miscellaneous foreigners making themselves at home. All Scots must unite for the total defense of Scotland in Scotland, under Scots control." At this point Sheriff MacDonald stopped Douglas from speaking.

The SNP printed the whole speech. It may surprise those who know only the British version of things. Douglas wrote:

> Your Lordship will have noted the frequent observations made by war-minded publicists that the population of Scotland is apathetic or unduly complacent with regard to the present hostilities. This is principally due to the obvious fact that the Scots are not fighting for any Scottish cause; we do not enjoy national independence, nor is the liberty of Scotland among the war-aims or peace-projects of the British and allied governments.... No intelligent Scot, of any age or sex, has any confidence in the British government; of the less intelligent Scots, at present somewhat numerous from various causes, more, in my judgment, have confidence in the government of the Soviet Union than have confidence in the British government (although I am far from suggesting their confidence is well placed).

Then, days later on April 23, 1942, Douglas came before Sheriff Sam MacDonald on a complaint of the Procurator Fiscal that he had contravened the National Service (Armed Forces) Act of 1939. Douglas argued a series of alternatives: that the Act was contrary to the Common Law of Scotland, which the Treaty of Union protected; that the Treaty of Union did not grant the British Parliament the right to draft Scotsmen; that the so-called British Parliament was in fact the English Parliament; that Great Britain had voided the Treaty of Union and as head of the Commonwealth of Nations was no longer an entity in international law, "since it had no exclusive undisputed control over all persons and things in its pretended territory, did not conduct its external relations independently of the will of all other states and did not give sufficient expectation of its permanence."

Sheriff MacDonald listened to Douglas' arguments, congratulated him on his learning, and regretted that he saw no second way but to sentence him to 12 months in prison. Douglas appealed to the High Court of the Justiciary and was freed on bail. In honor of his stand, he was elected chairman of the High Council of the SNP, a position he held until 1945. On July 9, 1942, he addressed to the High Court an hour-and-a-half version of his four objections. The court ignored all four and, in dismissing his appeal, ascribed to Douglas the contention, "All the acts of the Imperial Parliament since 1707 were void and of no effect," which he had not said. His legal objections were never adjudicated and, significantly, the proceedings were never published. He served eight months in prison (July 9, 1942 to March 10, 1943) and was released early for good behavior. Sorley MacLean wrote from Egypt that the only two places to be during the war were fighting the Nazis, as he was doing, or fighting the English, like Douglas. (He compared W. H. Auden, who had fled to safety at little Swarthmore College in the United States.)

Douglas emerged from prison, took a wife, and, as soon as his honeymoon was over, started contesting a by-election (held in February 1944) in Kirkcaldy Burghs in his native Fife county. He promised the voters that if elected he would work to give Scotland dominion status through a bill modeled on the British North America Act of 1867, which had created the Dominion of Canada. The Labour candidate, who supported Churchill's coalition government, expected little opposition from either Douglas or a pacifist who was running as a Christian Socialist. The Labourite won with 52 percent of the vote (8,268 votes), while Douglas received 42 percent (6,621 votes), a far cry from the virtual unanimity of which we hear in official accounts. An explosion occurred in the Cabinet. Ernest Bevin, the powerful head of the Transport and General Workers Union, a Labourite who was Churchill's Minister of Labour, insisted on beginning a new prosecution against Douglas, this time for opposing industrial conscription.

As the political pot boiled, Douglas meanwhile obtained
the signatures of the prime ministers of the various dominions
in favor of dominion status for Scotland. Most signed, including "the Liberal Mackenzie King, of Canada, and the Gaelic-
speaking Socialist Peter Fraser, of South Africa." One month
after the by-election, the Ministry of Labour summoned Douglas to be interviewed for a job in a munitions factory and
proceeded against him, when, as expected, he refused. At the
Sheriff-Court in Paisley on June 12, 1944, his case was heard by
Sheriff-Substitute A. M. Hamilton, "a rather deaf and testy old
gentleman, who kept interrupting and seemed not to understand what was said to him."

Douglas made several points. First, whatever the purported
omnipotence of the British parliament over Englishmen, its
authority in Scotland was limited by the Treaty of Union of
1707, which was meant to restrain the power of the central
government, as the United States' Constitution restrained their
federal government. Second, Article XVIII of the Treaty of
Union explicitly preserved Scottish Common Law in the area
of private right. This was indeed relevant to military conscription but was absolutely crucial in the case of the innovation
of industrial conscription. Douglas cited two cases, one from
English, the other from Scottish, law, in which a black slave
asserted his right to freedom. The English courts in 1707
found that *villeinage* was part of English law and refused to free

the slave. But the Scottish court in 1779 found that *villeinage*, serfdom, did not exist under Scottish law and freed the man. According to Douglas, industrial conscription was English Law applied to Scotland and thus violated the Treaty of Union, which preserved the validity of the rulings of the Scottish courts. Douglas also cited an Australian case. On May 25, 1944, the Supreme Court of New South Wales, Australia, had banned industrial conscription because it "imposed on the people the status of *villeinage*."

Third, Douglas argued that Parliament had no right to "delegated legislation," that is, to give to administrative bodies, such as the Ministry of Labour, the power to create and enforce their own laws. (This last point is still important to us, because the limitations the United States Constitution imposed on the central government have been circumvented by the creation of bureaucracies free to make, interpret, and enforce their own law.)

Douglas also praised Hayek's recent *Road to Serfdom* and denounced Socialists who wanted to keep industrial conscription after the war in the cause of full employment. "The slogan of Full Employment is appropriate only to a Servile State," he argued, referring to Hilaire Belloc's famous book. The Ministry of Labour's treatment of young Scottish women and of Douglas himself showed the dangers of such a system.

Douglas was found guilty and sentenced to three months

in jail. He appealed again to the High Court, arguing that both the act instituting industrial conscription and the enforcement of the act by the Ministry of Labor violated Article XVIII of the Treaty of Union. On October 6, 1944, the Court affirmed the earlier High Court ruling that Douglas was denying the validity of all acts of the British parliament since 1707. The Lord Justice-Clerk (Lord Cooper) interrupted Douglas with a series of questions until, by a slip of the tongue, Douglas assented to the charge that he had made a universal denial. Having confused Douglas into contradicting his written appeal, Lord Cooper sent Douglas to prison for three months, without hearing the appeal. There was much resentment of the government's actions, even among those who disagreed with Douglas' stand against military conscription, since it was clear that he was being harassed because of his good showing at the by-election.

"The question raised, " Douglas later wrote, "was, of course, that of federal constitutionalism, a question perfectly familiar to every American and Australian.... It was not enough for a sheriff or other judge to take refuge behind an Act of the Westminster Parliament if that Parliament itself had its powers restricted by an Act of two Parliaments, namely the terms of union, an international treaty, between Scotland and England. The English have been accustoming themselves to the dogma of the omnipotence of Parliament, but such a dogma is untenable in relation to Scotland, whose Parliament was never omnipotent, and is incompatible with the Treaty of Union which constituted the British Parliament to begin with."

Douglas saw the importance of Scottish nationalism for a federalist Europe. "Things are never settled until they are settled justly, and there will be no just or satisfactory international order in Europe till each nation of Europe has its due, equality of rights in its own affairs.... On this view my litigation about the Treaty of Union may be seen as a slight contribution to a rationally united Europe." Douglas foresaw a European parliament and, eventually, a world parliament, answerable to the world's national parliaments. In such a world, Scotland would need its own voice, that is, its own parliament.

He did not predict the formation of the current European Union, modeled on the omnipotent parliaments and bureaucracies of France and England. "The insular English, with their peculiar dogma that one is better without any rational constitution and that a legislature should be allowed to please itself and govern at discretion" are now entangled in both a European Union ruled by a European parliament and a Brussels bureaucracy free to impose laws on their helpless subjects, just as Westminster and Whitehall rule Scotland. Jacques Delors, in a speech to the European Parliament on July 6, 1988, predicted that 80 percent of all laws on economic, social, and fiscal affairs would originate in Brussels. It is no coincidence that among those who have said "no" to the European Union are the peoples of Norway and Serbia, chosen by Douglas as Scotland's peers in 1942.

The years that followed the war were filled with success and frustration. The unpopular Churchill government fell in a general election in 1945. In 1948, the SNP, up to then open to members of all parties or none, insisted that members of other parties resign. Hugh MacDiarmid, a Communist, and Douglas, a Labourite, resigned, although they had sat on the High Council.

Douglas turned to poetry and scholarship. His original poems in "Lallans," a name for the Scots dialect he took from Burns, led to an active role in the international writers' organization PEN, of which he was Scottish President (1957-1961). His translations of "The Twenty-Third Psalm of King David" and Valéry's "Cimetière Marin" were widely acclaimed and his theatrical versions of Aristophanes' "Frogs" and "Birds" ("Puddocks" and "Burdies") were performed at the Edinburgh Drama Festival.

As a scholar, he made important contributions to Greek classical codicology, the study of Greek manuscripts. His critical edition of Theognis in the prestigious Teubner series (1961) is still in print and remains of value because of Douglas' personal examination of the manuscripts and his notes on many passages. In *Chasing an Ancient Greek* (1950), a book about his trip to examine Greek manuscripts and visit the PEN congress in Venice in 1949, he explained why Theognis is worth reading. "Theognis had a mind of his own and spoke it, on matters of general as well as of personal interest. As such a spokesman he is a social and historical document of the first importance, all the more so that he is the most substantial relic of personal literature from the aristocratic particularist age, before Athenian national socialism and Macedonian dynastic imperialism." Douglas was describing himself in these words. During the last decade of his life, Douglas worked on the text and manuscripts of the Greek tragedian Aeschylus. For many scholars, Aeschylus is the engaged artist of the radical Athenian democracy, but not for Douglas. "Aeschylus was clearly a constitutionalist of the 'strict Constructionist' school who wished the supreme court to have the general guardianship of the democratic constitution so as to repress alike any tendencies to despotism or to anarchy."

Each time Douglas applied for a professorship in Scotland, he was turned down, despite impressive letters of recommendation. The great scholar of Greek religion, H. J. Rose, called him "without exception or doubt the most brilliant student I have ever taught." (In America, when confronted by obstreperous students, he would listen to their comments and then say, "H. J. Rose always said the best students disagree with their teachers.") In 1946, the chair at Glasgow went to A. W. Gomme, a senior scholar engaged in writing an important commentary on Thucydides. (He died before completing it.) Douglas taught Latin at University College, Dundee, but when in 1953 its Latin department was swallowed up by St. Andrews, he transferred to the Greek department of his old university. When he applied for the Greek chair there, however, Douglas was passed over in favor of K. J. Dover, a young Englishman of much promise, whose most important scholarship, which included helping to finish Gomme's commentary, began appearing in the late 60s. Dover liked St. Andrews, and a few years later turned down the offer of the Regius Professorship of Greek at Oxford to stay there.

If Douglas was unhappy about a Sassenach occupying a Scottish chair, no change in his cheerful disposition ever betrayed it. Dover is a fine scholar, but he does not suffer peers gladly. In his recent autobiography, *Marginal Comment*, he plays down Douglas' contributions to classical studies and harps on their scholarly differences, which were based on principle. (On the next page, however, he defends a nonthreatening, friendly colleague for mistranslating Latin.) He attributes to himself the growing popularity of Greek studies at St. Andrews in the late 50s and says the program had problems in the 70s because "I was beginning to lose my grip as a teacher." He does not note the interesting correlation between the program's ups and downs and Douglas' presence at St. Andrews. The most striking failures in Dover's career of almost unbroken success were his two chances to reach wider audiences, his Sather Lectures at Berkeley (1967) and his BBC show *The Greeks* (1980). Dover breathed a sigh of relief when Douglas left, and, having done his best work at St. Andrews, Dover returned to Oxford in 1976 as president of Corpus Christi College, where, by his own account, he seems to have spent much time hoping for the suicide of a difficult colleague.

After Douglas was turned down for the Greek chair at Aberdeen in 1965, he began to take seriously offers from America, finally accepting a position at McMaster University in Canada in 1968. The next year, he was appointed Paddison Professor of Greek at the University of North Carolina at Chapel Hill. He was as active and cheerful as ever, with no sign of resentment that he had become one of Ammianus Marcellinus' *Scotti per diversa vagantes.* He was popular with students and faculty and started writing one section of a major international commentary on Homer's *Odyssey.* On October 24, 1973, he missed a class and did not answer his phone. The Chairman of the Classics Department, George Kennedy, went to his apartment and found Douglas dead at his desk with copies of his own articles on Homer spread out on the table in front of him.

Douglas Young was a constitutionalist, a federalist, and a nationalist in an age of behemoth government, imperialism, and international power politics. He loved the languages and customs of the smaller nations of Europe—Serbia, Greece, Scotland—in an age when the great powers either ignored or trampled them. Since Douglas' magnificent political stands, the SNP has won seats in the British Parliament and has crippled the Conservative Party in Scotland. Poetry is still written in Lallans, though many would agree with Edwin Muir, "they never seemed to me to be very gifted, except for Grieve" (Hugh MacDiarmid). In the latest Scots anthology from Edinburgh, however, Douglas' name does not appear. Douglas' edition of Theognis is still in print and his articles are quoted. Fraenkel hated him, but Otto Skutsch, another refugee from Hitler who became Latin Professor at London, always beamed when Douglas' name was mentioned. Scholars came from all over the world to visit him at Chapel Hill, where he had time to direct only two dissertations (on the manuscripts of Aeschylus and Sophocles); the latter was written by me, the former by Dr. Thomas Fleming.

Douglas spent his 60 years fighting for lost causes: the restoration of the Scottish nation and its literature and the texts of ancient Greek poets. In his essay on F. H. Bradley, T. S. Eliot wrote, "We fight for lost causes because we know that our defeat and dismay may be the preface to our successor's victory, though that victory itself will be temporary; we fight rather to keep something alive than in the expectation that anything will triumph." Douglas' best known poem, which he used to hear quoted back to him on the hustings and at the market, contains his vision of what one man can accomplish. It is called "Last Lauch" (Last Laugh):

> The Minister said it wald dee,
> the cypress-buss I plantit.
> But the buss grew til a tree,
> naething dauntit.
> It's growan, stark and heich,
> derk and staucht and sinister,
> Kirkyairdie-like and dreich.
> But whair's the Minister?

Chapter XVIII

STILL IN SAIGON IN MY MIND

"The earth outside is covered with snow and I am covered with sweat. My younger brother calls me a killer and my daddy calls me a vet." This is the way the Vietnam veteran appears in a popular song recorded by Charlie Daniels (written by Dan Daley). The Vietnam War is over, but it is not settled in the mind and, more importantly, in the imagination of the American people. The official position on the war seems to enjoy a near-total consensus: the war was evil, the technocratic elite carelessly blundered, the Vietnamese people won a glorious victory because of the justice of their cause. Yet, in the rag and bone shop of the heart that provides the themes for popular art and entertainment, questions that editorial writers do not address echo and re-echo: How could such a strong and wealthy nation lose a war to a small and weak one? What happened to us in those days? What happened to our soldiers, the ones who hurried back and the POWs who came later and the MIAs who never came back?

Whittaker Chambers was able to discern little sense of tragedy in the American people. As a criticism of the intellectuals among whom he spent his younger days, the insight hits the mark. For the twentieth-century American intellectual, history is a train, subject to delays and strange detours, no doubt, but nonetheless moving steadily towards one far-off secular event. In this inevitable, mechanical progress, there may be backsliders and there will be martyrs, those who die for the cause, but the rightness of the cause and the inevitability of its triumph are assured.

The American people, on the other hand, live in a different sort of story—the world of an epic hero, Virgil's Aeneas. Aeneas loves his home, Troy, and fights to prevent its fall to the brilliant, tricky, and ruthless Greeks. After losing wife and home, he sets his sights on the future and journeys to Italy to found a new home for his people. There, at least for a little while, they are safe to build and grow again—until they must once more defend themselves against violence and trickery in themselves and others. But Aeneas knows that the losses are real and not so many Lenin-esque eggs broken for a glorious future omelet. *Italiam non sponte sequor.* "I am not going to Italy because I want to," Aeneas tells Dido. The deaths of brave young men represent real and irreparable gaps in the new state

Aeneas is founding. And still he goes.

The modern intellectual is like Hazlitt's Iago—one who cannot feel the desolation in the departure of each individual sacrificed for a future that is and must remain an abstraction. America's commitment to Protestantism and individualism indeed has its negative aspects, but that commitment does make Americans realistic. Americans can accept loss and sacrifice for what they are—loss and sacrifice. Whether he knows it or not, the typical American has had his mind formed on the hero who feels the loss and yet goes on to create. So the American is a kind of Aeneas; and the true American thus stands opposed to the martyr of the inevitable future, whether Ché Guevara or Martin Luther King.

The American popular imagination played with Vietnam themes that involve real loss and real sacrifice early on in the war. At the height of the war, John Wayne decided to make a movie modeled on the conventional epics that flowed out of Hollywood during the Second World War. *The Green Berets* (1968) is not a typical World War II propaganda epic, however. There is an enemy in Southeast Asia who is easily likened to the cold, barbarous Jap, a staple of the older films. But there is also an enemy at home. He is no second generation German, compromised into collaboration by a youthful indiscretion with the German-American *Bund*. The enemy is, rather, a newspaper reporter (David Janssen) who sneers at the good, blunt sergeant trying to explain to him the political realities of the conflict. The reporter is honest, though, and he accepts Wayne's invitation to see what Vietnam is really like.

The Green Berets was to prove prophetic in its themes. The question in Vietnam was not what was the war like—the evening television news was answering that question graphically. Rather, the question was, what was happening to the men who were serving there?

In World War II, the refugees huddled in Casablanca, waiting for the chance to escape. In Vietnam, however, the farmers and hill people tried to defend their own homes—and then in the night the Cong came to slay their leaders and teachers and parents. In *Green Berets*, we see an orphaned Vietnamese boy scourged by terrible loss—first the loss of his family; then of the honest South Vietnamese officer who subsequently tries to protect the boy; and, finally, the young American officer who, in turn, takes the youngster under his wing. Played by Jim Hutton, the officer is returning from a mission in which a young Vietnamese girl has sacrificed her virtue to capture a North Vietnamese general. He is caught in a trap and swung horribly into a grill of pungie sticks. The boy waits vainly for his new father to emerge from the landing helicopters. Then he and John Wayne walk off together along the beach. "After all, you're what this war is all about." One reporter is converted, one general captured, but the best are slain. There is little hope that the horror of emptiness will ever be erased from the young soul who has looked into the abyss.

It would be wrong to pass over the complex figure of Michael Cimino. Cimino has many contacts with the more popular aspects of the film trade and began his career working with Clint Eastwood, but he is committed to making artistic or "quality" films. In *The Deer Hunter* (1978), he focused on the healthiness of ethnic, working-class America, shaken, tortured, and, in some cases, tragically broken by the Vietnam War. The war was a kind of national suicide, and the theme of Russian roulette appears several times in the movie to underline this insight, from the gambling halls of Saigon to the POW camps of the North Vietnamese. The American Way of Life is, through it all, presented as a positive good—working, loving, and hunting. At the end, the remnants of the cast gather to sing "God Bless America." (Compare this with the somber and understated ending of *The Green Berets*.)

At the decade's end, however, Francis Ford Coppola's *Apocalypse Now* (1979) appeared. Though confused by the director's change from antiwar partisan to admirer of Nietzsche and power, the movie still emphasized the wildness, the craziness of the war. Martin Sheen is sent on a bizarre literary mission to assassinate a renegade U.S. officer, a reincarnated Kurtz from Joseph Conrad's "Heart of Darkness." Kurtz, played by Marlon Brando, stews in an Orson Welles-like obesity, worshipping power and death. His mission successfully completed, Sheen is haunted by the blood-thirsty climax of his task. Earlier in the movie we see Robert Duvall as a cavalry officer ordering a helicopter raid on a coastal village so that his new recruit from California can surf. Duvall's bravery in the midst of the whistling and exploding bombs is impressive, but we feel that it is an insane bravado. The movie-going public was told that the effect of serving in Vietnam was to make the soldier a dangerous nut. (In the original filming of the scene, Duvall manifested compassion as well as war-lust, by dashing through the shelling to rescue a deserted baby. Coppola cut the scene, to Duvall's publicly expressed disgust.) Likewise, on television, the stock villain, the greedy businessman, was being replaced by the outwardly normal and patriotic soldier who, on the inside, was an uncontrollable killer, broken by his participation in a criminal war.

While TV scriptwriters and movie reviewers applauded this vision of the Vietnam vet, the popular imagination was foster-ing another, as Cimino's *The Deer Hunter* suggests. Unfortu-nately few serious reviewers noted *Rolling Thunder* (1977), de-spite a script by Paul Shrader. William Devane starred as a POW returned to a hometown no longer his. His wife is bra-less ("No one wears them any more") and wants a divorce to remarry. Then hoodlums break into his house and brutalize him, al-though they cannot break him. He has, after all, been tortured by the Viet Cong. They do get to his wife and son and, after

robbing him, shoot them. Devane loses his family not to divorce and the new morality but to violence. When he recovers,
he goes hunting with a fellow POW, Tommy Lee Jones. At one
point, Devane takes a lover, who, scared by Devane's desire for
revenge, cries out, "Why do I always get stuck with the crazy
men?" He answers, "That's the only kind left." The film's climax, the annihilation of a Chicano whorehouse where Devane's
attackers are reveling, leaves the audience with disgust at the
sexual revolution and the new open society of the 60s.

Some have seen in *Rolling Thunder* yet another movie about
a Vietnam vet turned psychotic killer. They miss the gravamen
of the movie's charge against America: that those who fought
and suffered returned to find the country for which they fought
gone. Technically, it did not desert them; Nixon and Kissinger
got them out, all right. But their country is no longer their
own. The way of life they fought to defend has largely vanished.
The melting pot of America is a whorehouse.

Rolling Thunder succeeds in making us feel the main
character's resentment at this turn of events, so when, in the
end, the heroes limp away, embracing, after the completion of
their mission, the destruction of that whorehouse and its violent, degenerate inhabitants, we applaud. Or some Americans
do.

There are usually two angers in Vietnam movies. One, more
easily assuaged, is anger against THEM, the ones who sold us

out, whether in fighting a criminal war or in not letting us win it. At the heart of *Rolling Thunder*, however, boils the deeper resentment against the people who let slip from their hands the ideals for which the soldiers were fighting. In *Rolling Thunder* it is the ordinary Texans who have sold out. This resentment surfaced in spectacular fashion in Sylvester Stallone's surprise hit, *First Blood* (1982). Stallone's John Rambo screams, "Who are they to protest me?" His wrath is not directed against the elites. It is a small town in rural America that is blown away by Rambo. The rot in America is deep, and no superficial balm will quiet the throbbing cancer. The financial success of the movie was a surprise, but reviewers gave conventionally negative responses and chose to ignore the meaning of its popularity. They did not pause to ask themselves the question: Why would people, especially younger people, pay money to see such a picture when they stayed away from such artistic successes as Costa-Gavras' *Missing?*

The next Vietnam movie out was *Uncommon Valor* (1983), starring Gene Hackman. An aging officer whose son never returned from the war, Hackman is convinced that his son is still alive in Vietnam, held as a slave by the communists. In the face of official indifference, Hackman rounds up a group of Vietnam vets—many of them bizarre misfits, twisted by their wartime experience—and rescues a group of POWs and MIAs. Not his son, however, who had died for one of the survivors. The movie is moving, sensitive, far from abrasive, and the industry was caught by surprise at the audiences it attracted.

The success of *Uncommon Valor* did not escape the attention of Chuck Norris, a karate champ who had parlayed the early death of Bruce Lee into some money-making karate movies. Norris also saw himself as the true successor to John Wayne and seized the chance to succeed where Wayne had failed. In *Missing in Action* (1984), Norris plays a POW who escaped from an illegal Vietnamese prison camp and has now returned with an official U.S. delegation to uncover what the communists have been doing. There are some effective verbal confrontations, much action, some revenge, and a finale in which he breaks up a self-righteous Vietnamese media event by crashing in with a number of rescued POWs. Norris followed up *MIA* with a "prequel" on how his hero had escaped from the POW camp where he had been held.

This was the context in which Stallone did his own *MIA*-style film: *Rambo: First Blood II*. In this movie, Rambo is freed from the prison where he was sent after *First Blood*, in order to go into Vietnam to examine a carefully chosen empty POW camp. The bureaucrat who arranged this charade (Charles Napier) fouled up, however, because the camp is not empty. Rambo succeeds in getting a soldier to the rendezvous point—whereupon the bureaucrat declares the mission aborted and leaves Rambo and the rescued prisoner stranded. Rambo escapes and brings the men back with him, in the process killing an estimated 75 Vietnamese and Russians. Yes, Russians. The audience is left in no doubt about who is running the show in Southeast Asia.

The overwhelming financial success of *Rambo: First Blood II* awoke news commentators and editorial writers as well as reviewers from their dogmatic slumbers. When I saw the movie on Memorial Day 1985, every teenager in the audience got up at the end and applauded. The older viewers looked on in impotent amazement. In *Rambo*, Stallone has taken the hard-hitting motifs of earlier Vietnam movies and made them palatable for a mass audience. The American people are not to blame. Bureaucrats did us in. Given a chance, our men can stand up to torture and beat Charlie and his Russian master. For all its violence and movement, *Rambo* is ultimately a consoling film.

The defense of the American Way of Life against the enemy from the East was also the theme of another Vietnam movie by Cimino, *Year of the Dragon* (1985). In this film, Mickey Rourke plays a graying Vietnam veteran out to destroy a Chinatown drug lord with close and explicit ties to the drug traffic in Southeast Asia. Rourke is obsessed with the defeat in Vietnam, a defeat caused by cowardly and self-protecting bureaucrats. This time he is going to win, he says, almost in the very words of Stallone at the start of *Rambo*. The point is made again and again by Rourke himself and his closest friend. Few reviewers missed what the movie was driving at, and they were as angry as they were at *Rambo*.

Rambo's crusade kills many communists, but involves no serious loss to America. Even the treacherous bureaucrat survives. Rourke's victory, on the other hand, is costly, Virgilian. The bravest and truest of those around Rourke suffer. A brave, young Chinese-American policeman and Rourke's wife are both brutally slain. The beautiful Chinese-American TV reporter that he has lured into the investigation (and into bed) is brutally raped. But vicious cruelty cannot deter Rourke. *Year of the Dragon* is a fantasy, as much as Rambo is, but it is a much more mature fantasy. Virtue will triumph, but we are not allowed to shirk the cost of that victory. As in Virgil's *Aeneid*, a better society will emerge from the conflict, but the cost in human suffering and loss is real—and we must face them. In a world where easy and cheap success is promised from every TV screen and full-page magazine ad, this insistence on the cost of victory is needed by Americans as much as the enthusiasm and patriotism of Chuck Norris and Sly Stallone.

Movies are fantasies, but a nation's fantasies are also statements about itself. The fantasies of a good few filmmakers also seeped down into the television industry. In Stephen J. Cannell's lighthearted *Riptide*, serving together in Vietnam was shorthand for masculine loyalty and achievement. On the television program *A-Team*, serving together was somewhat more.

The A-Team is a group of twentieth century Robin Hoods, helping the downtrodden against the wealthy and the brutal. And why are they on the lam from the U.S. government? You have to listen carefully, but the reason is—because this crew invaded North Vietnam without (against?) orders. The invasion of North Vietnam is the great unspoken American fantasy. We could have won the war, if they had let us. This is the thematic undercurrent of most of the movies we have discussed. Movie and television critics, however, would rather talk about anything else.

The role of Vietnam in Glen Larsen's *Magnum P. I.* is more explicit and impressive than in other television programs. In this series Tom Selleck and his friends are Vietnam vets who have never really recovered from that experience. The three American buddies are successful enough in their own ways, and they love one another and are loyal to one another, but their careers and personal lives have been stunted by the war. Its disorienting horror touches them when they least expect it. In one episode, for example, a Vietnam medic has devoted his life to caring for the family of a friend who was killed in the war (though by drug dealers, not by Charlie), and his friend's wife and son have grown to love him. The woman wants to marry him. The former medic, however, is obsessed with revenge and, at the cost of his own life, assassinates the drug lord. Selleck finds it hard to explain to the woman why she had to lose the two men she loved. "You see, we shut our eyes and we forget. He shuts his eyes and he remembers." In 1984 Magnum returns with his whole crew to Cambodia to rescue the leader of the democratic resistance from the Vietcong. Here too the bravest—a young man, a wife, an old soldier—die, but when the others get back, they all agree that freedom is worth fighting for. They were right to go back.

The rational response to the totalitarian torturer and social engineer is surrender. Keep quiet and do things their way. The American people, however, found new heroes in the men who went through the frustration and defeat of Vietnam and who will not be fitted into that mold. For Americans, heroes are where you find them. No other people has taken policemen for their heroes, as we have and still do. We also admire the battered veterans of a lost war. Some, like Jim Stockdale and Dave Winn and Jeremiah Denton, are real heroes. Others are fantasies of the soldiers who fought in Vietnam, and, under their banners, the war goes on.

T. S. Eliot thought we fight for lost causes "because we know that our defeat and dismay may be the preface to our successors' victory." If the films that appeal to the popular imagination are evidence, the war is not over for many Americans—and so we are not yet defeated. What is more, Americans are willing to see abusive portrayals of the leadership that lost the war and brought on so many of the fruits of the 60s. You will not learn that from reading prestigious magazines and *New York Times* best-sellers; but the American people have discovered in the darkness of movie theaters and the privacy of their homes what they want to applaud, and they have begun issuing commands from the voting booth. The liberal Bourbons, who have learned nothing, are beginning to stir uncomfortably on their couches. The cries for equality and compassion that blare from the loudspeakers are being drowned out by a mob crying for excellence and victory, both personal and national. As yet, only popular art reflects this resurgence. Nevertheless, a satiated and sleeping elite may awaken one morning to discover that their cynical Vietnam misadventure brought on themselves a great popular revolution. "Sir," Rambo asks, "this time, can we win?"

Chapter XIX

PAYING AND PRAYING ON THE OLD HOMESTEAD

Farming "will remain the same though Dynasties pass," thought Thomas Hardy. In our own day, however, the farmer is beginning to be treated like a poor moulting bird whom tenderhearted environmentalists want the government to take under its wing. Hollywood became interested in the farmer and a spate of movies with well-known actresses appeared. The film establishment gave an Academy Award to Sally Field, and Jessica Lange won kudos from the critics. Then Field and Lange and Sissy Spacek and Jane Fonda went to Washington to testify before congressional committees about what they felt. Why?

The farmer enjoyed a short-lived success on the silver screen, because he was the latest addition to our nation's pantheon of victims. From time immemorial the farmer has been the one independent figure in our society. He can produce his own food and clothing. He can afford independence of views and action as no trader or professional can, because he can retreat back to his own land and grow his own food. He is the archetypical free man who, in Jefferson's vision of America, was the basis of a free society. But no more. Now letters to the editor, the suicide rate, and publicity all present him as a victim. Just as we have concerts to raise money for starving Ethiopians, so we have Farm Aid concerts for the farmer. He collapses into severe depression or explodes into violent outbursts. In *The River* he even sells himself as a strikebreaker to nefarious urban interests. The farmer is the puppet of forces he can neither control nor understand; whether big business in *River* or heartless bureaucrats in *Country*. The farmer wants to die and may well kill himself. He survives even in movie fantasy only because he has a star for a wife.

Jessica Lange's *Country*, Sissy Spacek's *The River*, and Sally Field's *Places in the Heart* (all 1984) together formed an instant genre, with its own conventions and stock motifs. There was the confrontation with the banker, at first businesslike, then moving straight to hostile, when wife and kids enter. There was the auction, beginning calmly and then degenerating into a shouting match between auctioneer and other farmers. There was the confrontation with bad weather, rain, or tornado. There was usually a scene with a woman struggling to handle machinery and finally succeeding (a sequence grotesquely mishandled in

River). Indeed, it was often hard to keep the scenes distinct in one's mind. Convention and motif are a part of all great art, but the predictability of themes in the farm genre was repulsive.

The source of the filmmakers' concern for farmers had tainted the stream. Film and television, as industries, are urban conglomerates. Their money comes from large urban companies. Scripts are written and then directed by city folk who live in L.A. or New York. On a trip to the country they feel like Spencer Tracy in *Bad Day at Black Rock* or Burt Reynolds in *Deliverance*—simple, straightforward souls from a peaceful, orderly city suddenly involved in the chaos and violence and dark mysteries of the rural world. This vision bears small resemblance to reality. It is our big cities that are chaotic and violent, while our rural communities live in comparative peace and order, the peace of the property owner, the natural order of the seasons. The born-and-bred city dweller feels more at home in the city than in the country. It is hard for him to notice the normal, and he is struck by the different, which he tends to interpret as the bizarre. The city dweller also tends to assimilate what he does see to what he knows. This leads to some striking insights and some appalling oversights. The most impressive insight is the vision of the modern farmer as a victim.

These films do reflect a dismal new reality. The farmer has joined the ranks of the bank teller who cannot talk back without losing his job or the honest cop who has to watch corruption flourishing. In the farm films, the banker is the farmer's friend and neighbor, but he, too, has his strings pulled by remorseless forces behind or above him, a monopolistic businessman in *River* or a ruthless bureaucrat in *Country*. The only way the banker can make things better is to quit. It is the vision of Wendell Berry's *Unsettling of America*. The farmer is, in many significant ways, a victim.

As we all are, to some extent. We live in a money economy. All of us, even the richest executive, depend on the artificial monthly or weekly doling out of money, not the natural creative rhythm of the land. We are all puppets of the sources of money: big business, big banks, big government. Even our freedom of speech is guaranteed only by these same sources. Inevitably we identify with the new, impotent farmer and rejoice in his or (in these movies) her rigged success against the money economy, just as we cheer Rambo and Rocky, when each takes up the fight against collectivist aggression. Cheering is good psychological catharsis, but in our hearts we know things do not work the way they do for Stallone's characters. We watch these movies on our VCRs or in darkened theaters, where it is hard to check up on us. On the job, in public, we keep our mouths shut and our noses clean.

All of us, you see, owe money to the bank or to credit card companies. We all feel frustrated at bureaucratic interference or the vagaries of a market economy, which even the experts fail to

explain and cannot control. In this environment the farmer has
become another film version of the secretary in *From Nine to
Five*, the factory worker in *Modern Times*.

But is the modern farmer only a victim, somebody due
only mawkish pity?

In the most recognizable stock scene of the genre, the man-
datory bank scene, the farmer has become something like a
Third World country that shouts at the banker that it was he
who urged the farmer to borrow the money in the first place.
Wilfred Brimley in *Country* has a few just words on this attitude. The farmers hired the money, didn't they? To depict the
farmer, of all people, as someone so out of touch with the
rooted nature of things as to believe the slick experts on economics, a group that has not been right since 1929 (to take a
year at random), is to present the modern farmer as infantile,
which he is not.

No. The farmer is not a victimized simpleton. In each film,
after all, someone fights back. Moreover, in each case a woman
with a family is behind it all. Here, too, is an insight that is
worth savoring. The basis of salvation and renewal in the secular world is family. Business can hurt a family as it does in
Country or even attempt to split it up, as it tries to in *Places*.
These films, however, depict the family—as they should—as the
basis for resistance to destructive and simplifying bigness.

And yet, is family enough? Common sense would say no.

Families need community. Only in *Places in the Heart*, however, do we see a real community at work. Rich and poor, healthy and blind, black and white work together to stop the seemingly inevitable loss of home and breaking up of community in the face of economic humiliation and racial hatred and sexual infidelity.

Places is also the only film in which religion, the bond of families, figures significantly. The narrative is framed by a church service. It begins with a father saying grace over a meal, and, in the final church scene, the entire community joins in the communion service: rich and poor, black and white, quick and dead. This scene is a picture of Paul's words—the church is the Body of Christ, the communion of true believers. That communion, that community, rooted in religion and protecting the family, is the true basis for the survival of home and farm. It is a powerful scene, incomprehensible to most urban Americans, Christian or not.

In the other films, religion is present but in weird forms. While *Places* begins with Field's husband, a strong masculine figure, giving thanks for the family's meal, women take turns in giving thanks in Jessica Lange's *Country*, the men in the movie being either old or broken by their lack of capitalist success. In *River*, Sissy Spacek has her children thank Sun and Earth for their food, the single phoniest scene in a movie reeking with phoniness. A list of reasons for success and failure could be lengthened, but in the end *River* and *Country* fail to give us a satisfying picture of the American farmer, because they lack a simple and sincere picture of his religion.

The inadequacy of *River* and *Country*, like the adequacy of *Places*, may best be judged by contrasting them with the rural vision portrayed in Peter Weir's *Witness* (1985). A Pennsylvania Dutch Amish child witnesses a brutal murder in Philadelphia's Thirtieth Street Railroad Station. Harrison Ford, the detective on the case, returns with the child and his widowed mother to the Amish country to hide them from the murderers. The Amish have separated themselves from hedonistic, capitalist America. They are thrifty and hard working pacifists, and they occasionally suffer from violent teenagers and rude tourists. They are free, however, and their freedom is rooted in community and religion. (They are also the one part of rural America unequivocally praised by Wendell Berry.) Saying grace is significant for the Amish. In one scene, Ford takes mother and child to a downtown fast-food joint and is literally biting into his hot dog, when the two bow their heads in silent prayer. He is frozen in embarrassment. Mouth agape, he stares at them. It is a funny and beautiful scene, and we are thus reminded of just how removed the urban American is from the natural response of most people, who thank God for His gifts.

Are the rural worlds of *Witness* and *Places in the Heart* mere fantasies? I did not find them so. They are needed reminders that the land, lovingly used and cultivated, can create culture as well as cultivation, character as well as crops. True productivity is rooted in a way of life and a way of life must have community and religion as well as family and personal success. The farmer should not be portrayed as a victim. It is not an honor he needs, just as he does not need his ersatz "rights" protected or the laws of economics turned upside down for him. All culture and creativity—I do not speak of productivity—are rooted in family, work, community, religion. To feel these things as alien, as many film people do, is to hate the human. We need to have less admiration for our *Audubon Society Magazine*, with its lovely scenes of nature empty of human presence, and more appreciation for our Grant Wood *American Gothic*. The businessman engaged in strip mining and the environmentalist zealously protecting empty spaces are closer than they think. Against them stands the farmer, user of the land, cultivator of it, worshipping and working with friends and family. He is a model of the truly human; and we cannot see that model too often.

Chapter XX

ARMS AND THE MAN: CLINT EASTWOOD AS HERO AND FILMMAKER

A nation lives by its myths and heroes. Many societies have survived defeat and invasion, even political and economic collapse. None has survived the corruption of its picture of itself. High and popular art are not in competition here. Both may help citizens decide what they are and what they admire. In our age, however, high art has given up speaking to the body of its fellow citizens. It devotes itself to technical displays that can appeal only to other technicians.

In the days of the great studios, Hollywood attempted to express a national feeling. This effort collapsed with the decline of the studio system in the 60s. (It is striking how many watchable films, along with a few masterpieces, the old system produced compared with the dated products of the 60s.) Yet the 60s did produce one filmmaker committed to films that both succeed as popular entertainment and speak to the American people.

Clint Eastwood's famous chipped tooth and limited acting range had slowed his career until he was cast as Rowdy Yates in the television series *Rawhide*. His youthful good looks and sullen passion won the hearts of the teenagers who were becoming the largest segment of the population in those years. Based on this success, Eastwood's agent got him a part in a European movie, a Western with Italians as director and villain.

A quarter of a century later, that villain, Gian Maria Volonté, is considered one of Italy's premier actors. And the director, Sergio Leone, is honored as the creator of one of the most popular sub-genres in film history, the "spaghetti Western." It is an education to watch Leone begin with *Per un pugno di dollari* (1964), hit his stride in *Per qualche dollaro in più* (1965) and go on to create *Il buono, il brutto e il cattivo* (1967). (I have little patience for his later, critically acclaimed movies. They resemble nothing so much as expensive imitations of Leone by someone who has studied Sergio Leone movies but cannot understand what made them work.) The original trilogy is slow paced but tense with excitement, superficially immoral but in fact deeply ethical. Above all, it has Eastwood. The men and the hour had met.

What Leone was doing needed Eastwood's strengths and could bypass his weaknesses. Leone needed a strong screen presence that was tough, had a sense of humor, and remained sympathetic, and Eastwood did not need to talk much. Critics scorned the films, and Italian Marxists explained that the trilogy and its many successful spin-offs were a Christian Democratic plot to make Italians forget about the economic troubles of the end of the Economic Miracle of the 50s. Ordinary people, however, flocked to see them and Clint Eastwood's screen persona was born, created by Leone's genius and Eastwood's own squinting charisma.

Leone saw an American West freed from the traditions and constraints of the Old World, open to incredible cruelty and violence, but ultimately saved by an individual with a moral center and a sense of humor. Critics noted the violence, horrific by the standards of the early 60s, but forgot that even if virtue was not always rewarded, honor and a sense of humor always triumphed over rootless evil. Eastwood never forgot what he learned from the Italian about pacing and humor, but above all he was struck by Leone's vision of the American West.

The late 60s, however, were not a good time for either man. Eastwood was cast in a number of Westerns, watchable now only because they include him. The nadir was the catastrophic *Paint Your Wagon* (1969), a musical Western that combined appalling immorality with unbelievably bad singing. Eastwood's walk through a forest singing, "I talk to the trees," may be the musical low point of a decade that listened to Herman's Hermits. The waste of money appalled Eastwood as much as the aimlessness of his career, and he finally founded Malpaso Productions so he could produce his own movies with complete artistic control.

The critical world howled with laughter at that proviso, but Eastwood proceeded to make a series of movies: sexy teasers like *Play Misty for Me* (1971), cop movies, and Westerns. It was the second type that won him the most enduring fame and that alienated the Hollywood elite. After more than two decades we can see *Dirty Harry* (1971) for what it is, a film masterpiece, the most influential work of popular art since *Uncle Tom's Cabin*. Although Don Siegel is a very different director from Sergio Leone, the Italian's vision of the American West can be felt in the film's ethical tensions.

Eastwood's own Westerns were made in the Leone mold. As the Italian's later movies became increasingly bizarre and out of touch with popular feeling, Eastwood's Westerns were the true continuation of Leone's project. In these movies, as in *For a Few Dollars More*, an act of immorality is avenged after a long time by a tough but honest hero. Even so, *The Outlaw Josey Wales* (1976) came as a surprise. Based on real incidents, the massacre of surrendering Confederate soldiers by Union armies at the end of the Civil War, *The Outlaw Josey Wales* has a title dripping irony. Wales has lost his family to Yankee raiders, a fact Eastwood brings home to the viewer by means of staccato flashbacks deployed with a power and control that Eastwood has not been able to recover. Wales refuses to ride down out of the hills to surrender to the Yankees—which means he witnesses the massacre of the Confederates at the hands of the treacherous Yankees. Wales charges and rescues one friend. That is why he is an outlaw. Flee-ing his relentless pursuers, Wales gathers around him a motley family of those who have suffered from the Union, including an Indian and some women who have lost their husbands and fathers. He finally establishes a new homestead and turns to face his tormentors. Directed with restraint and considerable humor, *Josey Wales* is now recognized as one of Eastwood's best movies, but he has been forgiven for it just as little as for *Dirty Harry*. There is no clearer statement that, in America, ordinary people can create a community without giving in to history's victors.

The picture of a true community that survives and prospers while at odds with the official society is found again in *Bronco Billy* (1980), Eastwood's most successful comedy and yet one of his most serious films. Bronco Billy's Wild West Show is Eastwood's vision of America. In one sense, it is a weird conge-ries of misfits, deserters, and losers. Bronco Billy, however, gives to these people the chance to create the world they need to live in. In fact, none of the members of the show is authentic. Not even the Indian is a real Indian. They are all fakes. They have, however, created their own personas, and in the final scenes, the show performs in a tent made up of American flags sewn by lunatics, and Eastwood tells the little "pards" to live up to the American ideals of law and order. The affirmation of his country and its mores manages to be splendidly absurd and deeply moving at the same time.

The French Hellenist Jean-Pierre Vernant said of Greek tragedy that it ceased using the tragic hero as a model and treated
him as a problem. The same change took place in the popular
art of the 50s and 60s, most strikingly in John Ford's later
Westerns, *The Searchers* and *The Man Who Shot Liberty Valance*,
and in John Le Carre's spy novels. Typical of the age were the
scenes added to *Patton* to cut the general down to size when it
became obvious that George C. Scott's *tour de force* performance
had made the general too heroic.

Eastwood's contribution, however, was to show how the
problematic hero could become a model again. Here, as in so
many other ways, *Dirty Harry* is crucial to the development. The
early scenes of the movie consistently show Harry breaking the
rules of sensitive, caring liberal America. We are deep into the
movie before we recognize with Harry's partner that Harry is
"dirty" because he is competent and so can be used to do all the
dirty jobs. Similarly, in *Bronco Billy* we learn only slowly that the
Wild West Show is a Potemkin Village for people who are not
really cowboys and Indians, but shoe salesmen and deserters. It
is nearly the end before we discover that creation of a new world
by people fleeing from a failed old world is the definition of
America.

Pale Rider (1985) is a likewise misunderstood Eastwood
masterpiece. Eastwood had borrowed key scenes from important movies before, but had never attempted a complete *mimesis*

of another movie. In *Pale Rider* he remakes *Shane* with an Eastwood avenger in the lead. Unlike *High Plains Drifter* (1973), where a corrupt community is destroyed by the avenger, the hero's revenge saves a community of miners, who face destruction at the hands of a corrupt and wealthy strip miner.

Eastwood's admiration for *Shane* is easy to understand. Alan Ladd is a man without family who saves not only a community, but also a family in the face of cruel violence and the temptations of adultery. That the family and the community are saved by a man who has been stripped of both is a constant Eastwood theme. Dirty Harry's wife was killed in a meaningless accident with a drunken driver. Josey Wales's family was destroyed by Union raiders. Bronco Billy shot his wife when he caught her in bed with his best friend. ("What did you do to him?" asks Sondra Locke. "Nothing," Billy replies. "He was my best friend.") In Eastwood the generic conventions of the Western unite with the motifs of epic. Eastwood's heroes are Virgilian. Like Aeneas, they have been stripped of family and city in order to lead others to a new home and a new community. *Josey Wales* and *Bronco Billy*, where these motifs are clearest, are, from the standpoint of art, Eastwood's most successful films.

These themes unite most perfectly in the final scene of *Dirty Harry*. Eastwood confronts an enemy whose madness, *furor*, will destroy society unless he is stopped—just as Aeneas confronts Turnus at the end of the *Aeneid*. The *Aeneid* ends with the death

of Turnus. Not so *Dirty Harry*. True, Harry disposes of the Scorpio Killer, but Harry also takes out his badge, throws it away,
and then slowly walks back, as the camera sweeps upward to
show us the hustle and bustle of the society for which Harry
will no longer risk his life.

The discarding of the badge and the leaving of the spineless
society are a direct *mimesis* of the end of *High Noon*—and are in a
way quite Virgilian. At some stage the hero will turn away from
weakness and corruption and devote himself to creating his own
community. That community may contain elements of the absurd, as in *Josey Wales* and *Bronco Billy*. The absurdity, however,
adds piquancy to man's stumbling search for honesty and honor.
The hero can no longer take refuge in his situation as a problem.
He must recover the harder and admittedly somewhat absurd
task of becoming again a model for healthy and honest people.

The dream of the West involves a frightened town, terrorized
by corruption and a guilty secret. That dream also contains the
promise of the frontier. It is a frontier in the human mind and
will, accessible to everyone with the courage and the honesty to
move out of corruption and weakness. Honesty and courage,
leading to creativity, are their own reward. They give meaning to
an individual and to a nation. In Eastwood's films, the troubled
American hero has ceased to be a problem and has become a
model. The Man With No Name is free to choose a name,
Bronco Billy or Josey Wales, and so are we.

Chapter XXI

PUBLISHERS AND SINNERS: AROUSING INTEREST IN THE CENTURY'S TOP 100 NOVELS

As the end of a century and a millennium loomed in view, responsible folk took a moment to reflect on the past. The most striking trend of the past thousand years was the growth in creativity, influence, and prestige of distinctively Western institutions, including, although hardly limited to, science, politics, and the Christian churches. Even those, within and without the boundaries of the West, who found something—or much—to criticize in these institutions still used them. Of the largest and most influential Eastern nations, Japan and India have multiparty democracies (although historically with one dominant party), while China is a Marxist People's Republic. Even if we call the last regime a tyranny or dictatorship, we are still using Greek and Latin words and Western concepts to talk about these governments and we continue to judge them by Western standards. President

Clinton, during his friendly visit to Communist China, insisted on referring to freedom of speech and religion as universal human rights, although even a dropout from the Politics curriculum offered to Rhodes Scholars at Oxford ought to know enough history to realize that these concepts are far from being universal. They are the invention of one of the earth's many cultures. The growing Japanese, Indian, and Chinese economies are founded not on those nations' traditional technologies, as impressive as they were, but on Western technology based on Western science. Old China could build the Great Wall, but today's Marxist China is interested in an aerospace industry learned, borrowed, or outright stolen (with the probable connivance of the Oval Office) from the United States. Much the same could be said of the Japanese television industry or India's growing computer industry. None of these countries has converted to Christianity, although liberalism and Marxism can be analyzed as secularized Christian heresies, complete with sacred texts, inspired prophets, brave martyrs, and apocalyptic kingdoms. All of them date the closing years of the century from the work of a sixth-century monk, Dionysius Exiguus, who created a chronology based on the birth of Jesus, a date he came very close to getting right.

The most striking trends of the past hundred years, on the other hand, have been the suicidal wars which marked them and the growing criticism of those Western institutions which seemed so dominant at the beginning of the twentieth century. As we have seen, multiculturalists use the enormous expansion of the prestige of Western culture as a counter intuitive argument to stop studying Western culture in the original languages and replace that study with superficial surveys of other cultures. According to the multiculturalist argument, the popularity of Western technology and the riches of the global economy make a multicultural One World inevitable, whether we want it or not.

Every society has tools and ways of satisfying basic needs. To use words of Greek origin, as our society likes to do, every society has technology and economics. The society's culture, its religion and way of life, once determined how its technology and economics would help it obtain what it wanted from life. It is only in the past two hundred years or so that a popular theory emerged arguing that we should do whatever we can do—that instead of our directing technology, our technology should direct us. "Things are in the saddle and ride mankind," was Emerson's way of expressing it.

> There are two laws, discrete
> Not reconciled—
> Law for man, and law for thing;
> The last builds town and fleet,
> But it runs wild,
> And doth the man unking.

Western science, technology, and politics (republican, liberal, or Marxist) are the creations of Western culture, the fruits of what Yeats called a "great-rooted blossomer." The tree of Western culture will be able to keep on producing those fruits only if it is nurtured by people who have worked long and hard to master the skills and knowledge needed to maintain that tree. The technocrat, the multiculturalist, and the postmodernist have declared war on the long and difficult course of study and acculturation needed to participate in the tradition that produced the science, technology, and politics that so many want.

Do they really want them, however? Or do they want only the many bright, sparkling things that are produced by them? Do they want the American culture of the Founders, rooted in English Common Law, Greek and Latin literature and political thought, and Protestant Christianity? Or do they just want to see violent, R-rated American movies?

As the century creeps to its close, the producers of American culture, in the narrow sense, of American books and movies, looked back over the twentieth century to see what they had wrought. In 1998 they presented the American public with several sets of the 100 best movies and books of the twentieth century. The American Film Institute in Hollywood arranged for the best movies to be voted on by 1,500 leaders of its field. A division of Random House publishers called The Modern Library asked its editorial board, a group of American intellectuals of a predominantly leftist cast, to draw up a list of the 100 best novels in English. The Modern Library also went to Radcliffe, a prestigious women's college, and invited 100 students at a summer course on publishing there to vote on a list of their own. Both these votes were based on a pre-selected list of 400, drawn up by the Modern Library editorial board. Meanwhile in England, ordinary Britons were asked to vote on their favorites. (So far nobody has voted on the 100 best American poems of the century, or paintings or buildings. Ten would seem a more plausible number and cultural standards have become so confused that it is perhaps not very likely that a consensus could be reached even on that low number.)

Both Hollywood and the Modern Library had financial reasons for their ventures—to encourage people to buy copies of the chosen movies and books. The idea worked. The day after the Modern Library announced that Joyce's *Ulysses* was the best novel of the twentieth century, 80 orders for the book came in, about a quarter of sales for an entire year. The attention the marketing devices attracted shows, however, that some people still feel that what we read or ought to read helps us to describe ourselves. Granting that they are right, what do we look like?

Let us look at the novels first. The American intellectuals' choices were closer to the Radcliffe girls' list than to the ordinary Briton's. The American men chose Joyce's *Ulysses* as the best book of the century. The Radcliffe girls voted for F. Scott

Fitzgerald's *The Great Gatsby*, while the British readers voted for Tolkien's *Lord of the Rings*. The groups were not always so far apart. *The Great Gatsby* was first with American college girls, second with American intellectuals and twelfth with the British. George Orwell's *1984* and *Animal Farm* came right after Tolkien in England and are numbers 9 and 17 on the Radcliffe list. The intellectuals put them in their list, as numbers 13 and 31. The intellectuals' list had no children's fiction, while there were a number of books originally written for children on the Radcliffe and British lists. The first choice of the ordinary Britons was on neither American list. Joyce and Tolkien seem so disparate that it may be worthwhile thinking about them.

The Classical influence is strong on both *Ulysses* and *Lord of the Rings*. Joyce's novel is explicitly a retelling of Homer's *Odyssey*, while Virgil's *Aeneid* was a central, if less explicit, influence on Tolkien. Both works were the result of extensive scholarship, some mainstream, some idiosyncratic, and took a long time to write. Both works tried to show ordinary people struggling to live their lives with heroic story patterns hanging over them, patterns which encourage them at times but also judge them.

For the common reader the differences will seem greater than the similarities. Tolkien's *Ring* trilogy is profoundly traditional in mood, themes, and technique. Joyce's *Ulysses* is overflowing with literary innovation. I would have called it the *ne plus ultra* of literary modernism, had he not gone on to write *Finnegan's Wake*. It is hard to think how much further innovation can be carried if the work is to be at all readable. I suspect the recipients of the 80 copies of *Ulysses* ordered after the publication of the Modern Library list were more than a little nonplused when they actually tried to read it. I knew a novelist, John Ashbrook, who tried to advance beyond Joyce in technique with a novel, *The Mountain and the Feather*, which he wrote in the second person. You, the reader, are described as living, enacting the plot at every step. After only a few pages, you feel like throwing the book down and shouting, "No, dammit, I did not do that!"

Ulysses, William Faulkner's *The Sound and the Fury* (6), and Malcolm Lowry's *Under the Volcano* (11) are high on the intellectual's list. The Radcliffe list ranks *Ulysses* number 6 and *The Sound and the Fury* number 10. It is fair to wonder whether these books are much read outside of colleges and universities. (Naturally, creative writers draw on them for their own work.) It is probably no accident that the juvenile book trade is so marked a presence in the lists voted on by ordinary readers. Modernist art is technically experimental but ethically out of touch with ordinary people's hopes and fears. (It is frequently downright disgusting.) Children's literature cannot afford to lose touch with its readers. Once upon a time English majors could be forced to read challenging modernist literature, but

with the dramatic drop in English majors in the last generation, the animals are increasingly running the zoo of the university English curricula, which seem to favor detective stories and
Westerns over experimental *tours de force*. (I once met a B.A. in
English from Duke's prestigious postmodernist English department who told me her favorite course there was on *The Godfather*.)

A good sample of what goes on in classrooms before college can be gleaned from *dear author*, a book of letters written as
assignments by junior high and high school students to their
favorite authors, living and dead, as part of a program set up by
Our Weekly Reader magazine and the Library of Congress' Center for the Book. Unlike the top 100 lists, the students tell us
why they chose the books they write about.

Mark Mattox of Portage, Michigan, hurt his foot jumping
on a trampoline and was stuck at home for two weeks. In bore-
dom he began to read Johann David Wyss's *Swiss Family Robinson*.
Mark loved the book and wrote, "Mr. Wyss, you have certainly
succeeded in making an incredibly sad environmentalist out of
me. Your work is definitely one of the strongest outcries against
pollution and overpopulation I have ever seen, heard, or read
in my entire life; what is contained within your book is an
entire world that our self-centered race has taken up in its massive hand and squeezed to a cruel and unneeded death." Mark's
letter is a tribute to the success of our educational system. Where

I remember a fast-paced tale, full of adventure, danger, and loyalty, a well-trained catechumen in our schools finds a strong cry against pollution and overpopulation. Unlike the old New Critics, who rejected moralizing interpretations of literature, these bright students find morals everywhere, including morals the authors could not have intended, as with Wyss. Usually, however, they are right about what the authors and their teachers wanted them to learn.

Linetta Alley of Bridgewater, Virginia, thanked Bette Green for *Summer of My German Soldier*. "This book gave me such a different perspective on how prejudiced our country is." This seems to be the main lesson our schools are teaching to fill up the hours left vacant by the abolition of foreign language instruction and the shrinking of time devoted to mathematics. Ginger Bradeen wrote to Lois Lowry, "I live in a small town in Oregon, where I see bigotry, prejudice, and discrimination every day." Astum Khan of Rolling Meadows, Illinois, wrote to Alex Haley to thank him for *The Autobiography of Malcolm X*. "I was Indian and Muslim, and everyone knows how Americans feel about those who are different. You are an outsider. A stranger. Nobody wants you. You can make as many white friends as you want, but when it comes right down to it, they're American; you're not." It is reassuring to see how grateful recent immigrants are for our immigration policies.

For American students, politics are, in Thomas Short's

phrase, "Oppression History." Out of 75 letters, two are to Alex Haley, two to Anne Frank, and three to John Steinbeck. Books on the Holocaust receive five letters, including Jane Yolen's *Briar Rose* and Jerzy Kosinki's *Painted Bird*. Emily Judge of Wheaton, Illinois, wrote to Elie Wiesel, "I was assigned to read *Night* and literally groaned when I discovered it was about the Holocaust. I felt that I had heard enough about that terrible time period and didn't understand why teachers persisted in making me read such graphic accounts.... As I finished the book, I threw it across my room, angered and disgusted." Eventually Emily repents and there is a happy ending. "Thank you for the courage you had to write *Night*. Never again will I shut myself off from reality." James A. Booms of Ubly, Michigan, wrote to Leon Uris, "I can relate to the peasants in the *Trinity* book in many ways. Like them, I am growing up in a farming village, I am Catholic, and I too feel the pressure of foreign rule. The major difference is that my foreign rule is my parents and the teachers who grew up in a different world." I did not find any letters to Madison or Tocqueville thanking them for making sense out of our political system, or to Winston Churchill for telling the story of the English-speaking peoples.

Despite a common impression, religion is not totally lacking from the American public school system. *dear author*'s index includes entries for "Judaism" and "Muslim." The entry, "ancestors," refers to a letter by Betty Chu of San Francisco thanking Laurence Yep for his *Child of the Owl*. "Now I understand why my mother prayed to my ancestors with me," she writes. The absence of an entry for "Christian" in the index is a slip, but perhaps not an accident. Lacey Murphey writes to thank Janette Oke for *The Calling of Emily Evans* because the book helped Lacey in her decision to become a missionary. The letter mentions church and Vacation Bible School. Breeann Songer of Ellicottville, New York, is more discreet in her letter to Madeleine L'Engle. "From your books I can tell that you believe in God and His ways the same way I do. I thought it was wonderful when you said He makes sure each star has a name so they won't feel unwanted." The Christian authors do not seem to have been read as school assignments and so are exceptions to the general rule.

This may explain why no student writes to C. S. Lewis to thank him for trying to puzzle out a rational basis for religious faith. An emotional response to oppression is at a premium in American public schools. Brad Lockard of Jackson, Kentucky, did write to Jim Garrison to thank him for teaching him to question authority. "By the time I finished the book, I had formed my own opinion: the government helped to kill Kennedy.... Your book inspired me to challenge even *your* view on the government and the assassins." Bill Campbell of Flint, Michigan, learned from Niccolò Machiavelli not to trust politicians. The banality of their conclusions is disappointing, but at least the young men are trying to think.

These young people, whether thinking or emoting, are confronting ethical issues in the works they read. The attack on the ethical dimension in literature was the great achievement of the liberal regime in America, symbolized by the abolition of most legal censorship and the rise of the technical literary criticism and theory that has driven literary scholarship to the fringes of the Groves of Academe. The result was predicted and came: the dominance of the R-rated movie, the pornographic Internet site, and the modernist novel. Many older readers and viewers have simply given up on recent novels and films. "Enough!" they say. They may reach their limit with works of artistic merit, like Cormack MacCarthy's *Blood Meridian* or Quentin Tarantino's *True Romance*. Or it may be the constant moral sewer of episode after episode of popular television shows that drives them back to older books and movies. They start to wonder: Why were so many more good movies made in the thirties and forties? Why were so many more good novels written in the nineteenth century than in the twentieth? Of course, there are several factors, but one keeps reoccurring. Unlike today's books and movies, they were written under censorship.

Neither violence nor sex is lacking in classic works of literature. The *Iliad* and the *Odyssey*, to go back to the origins, depict violence and mention sex over and over again. So does the Bible, as old fashioned American atheists used to point out. These acts, however, form part of works which had a moral purpose. Often the moral context was explicit, as it is in the Bible. The first scene in the *Odyssey* does not begin with Odysseus, but with Zeus, who proclaims that moral right and wrong exist, that the gods support the right and that wrong doers will be punished eventually. Zeus does not talk that way in the *Iliad*, but the ethical dimension appears again and again. In Book Three when the Trojan Pandarus tries to murder Menelaus after Menelaus has beaten Paris in a duel fair and square, King Agamemnon proclaims, "Now I know that holy Troy will fall!" When Achilles rejects the offers of the Greek ambassadors in Book Nine, Ajax denounces him for repudiating the rules that make human society function, and Achilles acknowledges that Ajax is right. Even more powerfully in Book Twenty-four, the gods intervene to stop Achilles from desecrating the body of his great rival, Hector. Later, Achilles looks on Hector's old father, Priam, and realizes that his father, too, will some day mourn his son. There are rules and limits and they apply to him, too. That is the moral lesson that the criminal and the tyrant, ancient Greek or modern American, will not accept. Old novels and old movies are full of that moral and that is one reason why they still attract an audience, while their more recent competition becomes dated so rapidly.

A vision of life that insists that there are rules and limits—and that they apply to you—informs most ancient literature.

Sometimes it is implicit, as with Homer's Achilles or Sophocles' Ajax. Often it is explicit. The lyric poet Pindar in the fifth century B.C. repeats this lesson over and over again to the wealthy aristocrats whom he praises in his poems. In the next century Aristotle reminded his readers of this truth in his *Ethics*. His teacher, Plato, taught, "Man is not the measure of all things." Contrary to what the fifth-century Sophist, Protagoras, thought, "God is the measure of all things." In the great choral ode on man near the start of Sophocles' *Antigone*, the chorus sings about man who can conquer even Mother Earth and cure every disease, but he cannot cure death. Yet the true modernist accepts no limits in art, science, or life. He is convinced that we can cure even death, if enough resources, money, and man-hours are spent on the project.

The modernist believes that there are no limits, because there is no limiter. "If there is no God, all is permitted," Dostoyevsky saw. He wrote great novels in a century when great novels could still be written. Tolkien continued the tradition of the nineteenth century, as well as of earlier centuries. God is not mentioned in *Lord of the Rings*, but its author was a Christian and a traditionalist attempting to evoke the moral mood of *Beowulf*, a work about a time before Christianity written by a Christian. In the United States, its readers are often said to be members of the counterculture. In Italy the *Lord of the Rings* is a favorite of the traditionalist right. They see that the *Rings* trilogy is not only a civilized book, it is a civilizing book. It belongs to the tradition that began with the *Iliad* and *Odyssey* and is still alive—"the ever defeated, never altogether subdued side," as Tolkien wrote to his son.

Joyce's *Ulysses* is the true epic of the twentieth century because it takes up the elements of the great tradition of the Greek and Latin classics and their later European successors and puts them in a new context. It is a context where the artifacts of the past still survive, but not the living tradition that makes sense of those artifacts. George Orwell understood this when he wrote *Inside the Whale*. "What Joyce is saying is, 'Here is life without God. Just look at it!' and his technical innovations, important though they are, are there primarily to serve this purpose."

Ulysses is not only a rewriting of Homer's *Odyssey*, like Virgil's *Aeneid*, it is also a rewriting of Dante's *Comedy*. The *Odyssey* begins with Zeus proclaiming that at the end of the many and confusing roads a man might take, he will have to answer for what he chose to do. Dante's *Comedy* introduces Virgil to lead Dante and us through what seems a chaotic and meaningless labyrinth of horrors and suffering, but which we learn is a carefully structured artistic and moral whole. With God's help we can escape from the horror and the suffering and find joy and meaning. Joyce in *Ulysses* makes us confront what is left of tradition and culture in the Enlightenment world. They are the flotsam and jetsam from the wreck of a great ship which has floated up on a desert shore to amuse, instruct, or bore us.

The *Odyssey* once ended with Odysseus reunited with his true peer and soul-mate, his wife, Penelope, and now ends with the divine restoration of civil and moral order in Ithaca. Dante's *Comedy* ends with the human soul achieving true fulfillment in the contemplation of God, who is not only the Truth but also the Love that moves the sun and the other stars. *Ulysses* ends with a woman agreeing to have sex with a man. "yes I said yes I will Yes!" Without God, without the transcendent, nothing else is left. In Plato's *Symposium* Socrates learns that human sexual desire is a clue, a physical sign to lead the human soul to true fulfillment. Molly Bloom's unpunctuated interior monologue was added to the completed *Ulysses* just as Book Twenty-four was added to the *Odyssey*. Its male counterpart is the last scene of the cruelest and most honest of Hollywood movies, *Carnal Knowledge*, directed by Mike Nichols from a script by Jules Feiffer. The male, played by Jack Nicholson, has no culture, though he attended a prestigious college. He has no wife or children, although he has slept with many women, including his best friend's wife. He is the liberal counterpart to the revolutionary described by Emiliano in Steinbeck's *Viva Zapata!* "You have no farm, no land; no wife, no woman. You have no love. To destroy—that is your love!" With all their similarities there is a difference between the liberal and the Communist. The Communist still has a world to change or wreck. The liberal ends up with nothing left worth wrecking. In the last scene of *Carnal Knowledge*, Jack Nicholson visits a woman who is paid to arouse him one more time. After a lifetime of freedom that experience is all that remains, and it is worth any price, any shame, any betrayal. That is the truth seen by the most clear-sighted of all liberal philosophers, William Jefferson Clinton. He is the Socrates of the twentieth century, as Joyce's *Ulysses* is its *Odyssey* and *Comedy*. In the last scene of his *Comedy*, Dante contemplates God, who moves all things by his Love. The liberal contemplates himself aroused one more time by loveless contact. Aristotle's God was the Unmoved Mover, who moves all things without himself being moved. The liberal is the object of sex without himself having sex. "Here is life without God. Just look at it!"

Chapter XXII

THINGS YOU SEE BETTER
IN THE DARK:
THE FATE OF AMERICAN CINEMA

The American Film Institute (AFI) presented its list of the 100 Best American Movies in 1998, just as The Modern Library published its list of 100 Best Novels in English. Although marketing lurked behind both maneuvers, the creation of these lists shows that even the liberal tradition of anti-traditionalism feels the need for a canon, a list of approved texts that embodies and exemplifies what the liberal regime stands for. If the AFI had been truly loyal to liberalism's democratic ideals and plutocratic reality, it should have ranked the movies on the basis of the amount of money they earned in steady dollars. Everybody who had ever paid to see a movie would have had a vote. (The French count the number of seats sold, which is a more objective way of measuring a movie's popularity, because it eliminates the bias of inflation.) The thought of *Gone With the Wind* nudging past *Citizen Kane* and *ET* jostling ahead of *Schindler's List* was probably too much for Hollywood's image-conscious leadership to contemplate. So the list was "selected by AFI's blue-ribbon panel of more than 1,500 leaders of the American movie community," in the words of the official press release. These leaders included talk show host Larry King and President Bill Clinton. (Presumably, if you are the leader of the free world, you are also one of the "leaders of the American movie community.") When the list was presented on television, we got to hear various members of the panel introduce their favorite movie. President Clinton, for instance, said that his favorite was *High Noon* (voted number 33). Since the President lives by the public opinion polls, some find it hard to understand what he sees in a movie about a marshal (Gary Cooper) who does his duty, no matter what other people do or say. They may understand the movie's appeal to the President, however, when they remember the scene where Cooper's wife, Grace Kelly, saves her husband's life by shooting an enemy in the back.

The MGM lion used to roar through a wreath on which were inscribed the words *ars gratia artis*, "art for art's sake," in Latin. It was never purely for art's sake, of course, and money always mattered more than art. The temptation to drag the subject and the audience down to the level of the lowest common denominator was present in Hollywood from the beginning. In 1934 the Hays Office began its work, and it was under the censor's watchful eye that most good American movies were made. *Birth of a*

Nation (1915) and *Godfather* (1972) are among the exceptions to the general rule that the best Hollywood movies were made when they were censored. Hollywood's decision in the late 60s to give up on family films and charge more for teenage boys to watch violence and pornography was a fateful decision, but a natural one once the censor's restraining leash was removed. The film industry believed that R-rated films would make more money, and that self-fulfilling prophecy has come true as the audience for mature and intelligent films fled theaters in disgust. (Even so there are still years when G and PG movies dominate the top 5 money makers.) When we look up from the bottom line, however, we see that there are so many degrading films because the kind of people who control the making of movies like them. Mature and thoughtful people often find themselves unable to watch recent movies. Those who do watch them develop a taste for them. Alexander Pope predicted the progress of the American movie in the eighteenth century:

> Vice is a monster of so heinous mien
> That to be hated, needs but to be seen.
> But seen too oft, familiar with her face,
> We first endure, then pity, then embrace.

The AFI list is like a college catalogue. You can get a liberal education at most, or at any rate, at many American colleges and universities, but without informed advising the average student is not likely to find the right courses. There is the same difficulty in finding the good movies on the AFI Top 100. Of course, European films had to be eliminated. The best of Europe would have left only a few American movies among the top twenty. I would have eliminated most of the films of the past 30 years on the list. For a serious picture of an American businessman, *Dodsworth*, with Walter Huston's outstanding performance in the title role, belongs in the top 20. (The novel *Dodsworth* belongs among the top 100 American novels much more than the dated satire of *Main Street* and *Babbitt*.) The comic parallel to *Dodsworth* is *Life with Father*, with William Powell in the title role. *The Prisoner of Zenda*, with Ronald Colman and *Now Voyager!* with Bette Davis belong in my top 100, not to mention *Viva Zapata!* All combine excellent acting, good writing, and moral high seriousness. The AFI put Disney's *Snow White* and *Fantasia* on its list. Both movies are technically distinguished, but neither shows the character and maturity of *The Lion King*.

The American Film Institute's blue-ribbon panel decided that *Citizen Kane*, the brain child of the young Orson Welles, is the best Hollywood movie of the past hundred years. Like *Ulysses*, which was chosen by the editorial board of the Modern Library as the best novel of the same period, its technical innovations flabbergasted audiences when it first appeared and are still impressive after two generations of imitation. It is less impressive on other levels. The secret behind a great democratic leader's overweening ambitions and self-destructive behavior as businessman, politician, and husband turn out to be the fact that he was taken away from his mommy when he was a child. This may have seemed brilliant in 1941, but looks reductionist and even simpleminded today as Dr. Freud's influence wanes at the century's end. *Citizen Kane*'s phenomenal technical innovations and striking camera angles are less dated than its attempts to reduce political and industrial achievement to the psychology of the spoiled child. (To give the Devil his due, I used to believe that no one who could rise to political prominence would be likely to risk it all for a tawdry love affair. History has taught me to appreciate Orson Welles's prescience.)

Walter Huston's portrayal of Dodsworth provides a truer picture of an American businessman. Dodsworth has created a successful business which manufactures high quality automobiles and then, under pressure from his wife, sells the business to a larger firm to enjoy the fruits of success. He did not inherit his business, like Charles Foster Kane, and does not use it to attract attention to himself. He is a man who is fulfilled in work. Cut off from his mission, first his marriage and then his life go downhill until he meets a woman who teaches him what he really is and he decides to go back to work. *Dodsworth* is our best film portrait of an American man. Even *Dodsworth*, however, is not so great a film as Francis Ford Coppola's *Godfather* (number 3 on the AFI list).

The Godfather is Don Vito Corleone (Marlon Brando), the leader of a barely assimilated immigrant people in a hostile land. He became a criminal in American society in order to preserve his family and his people. With all his power, however, he has no true heir. His oldest son, Sonny, is likable and charismatic but erratic and unable to control his temper. His second son, Fredo, is a weakling, physically and mentally. The Don adopted Tom Hagen, who is bright enough, but not a Sicilian. The Don's youngest son, Michael (Al Pacino), is a natural leader, but wants to become a mainstream American.

In the second of his great Pythian odes for the Greek tyrants of fifth century Sicily, Pindar tells Hieron of Syracuse, "Learn who you are and become it." That is the progress of Michael Corleone. He learns and accepts who he is after a failed attempt to assassinate his father. (The Don is shot for refusing to give protection for drug trafficking because he thinks it is "un' infamia," a moral obscenity.) When Michael visits his father at the hospital, all his bodyguards are gone, ejected by a crooked policeman. He moves his father to safety and when the wounded old man wakes up, he tells him "I'm here, father." Brando nods silently and a tear streaks down his face. Michael tells him, "Father, I'm with you now." At first hearing he seems to be repeating comforting words. In fact, as we learn, he is announcing his decision to give up his chance to use his reputation as a war hero to join the American way of life. Instead, Michael has decided to stay with his family and his people as the leader they need.

The relationship of the Godfather to his followers is that of the ancient Roman patron and his clients, as we find it portrayed in Roman history and presented by such classics as Lily Ross Taylor's *Party Politics in the Age of Caesar* or Ronald Syme's *Roman Revolution.* The ancient Roman *cliens* was linked to his *patronus,* not by money, but by favors, acts of loyalty. Even a patron's defense of his client in court was looked on as a gift offered out of friendship. It was illegal under Roman law for a patron to receive money in payment for that favor. This relationship is still alive in the famous first sequence of *Godfather,* where the Americanized Italian immigrant, Amerigo Bonasera, comes to Don Corleone to ask for revenge on the powerful WASPs who beat up his daughter. The Don, like an ancient Roman *patronus,* rejects Bonasera's offer of money as an insult. "Some day, and that day may never come, I will ask you for a favor." American Founders like Thomas Jefferson read the *Tusculanae Disputationes* and *De Officiis* and admired Cicero the philosopher. Don Corleone never read a line of Cicero, but lived the way of life of Cicero the patron.

For the modern American the relationship between men is ruled by the cash nexus. A policeman or a teacher, even a called and ordained minister of the Gospel, will say of this or that act, "That's what I am paid to do" or "I'm not paid to do that." Of course, in real life, the care of the dissertation director or the political boss and the loyalty of the graduate student or the ward-heeler is still important, perhaps even crucial. The Roman and the *mafioso* are frank about what we disguise. Even when we act out of religious vocation or personal loyalty, we proclaim that we are doing it for money.

Even more confusing for the modern individualist are the areas where the tradition insists on money—for example, the giving of a dowry when a daughter is married. The individualist marries out of personal affection or sexual attraction. In the tradition, marriage unites families, not just individuals, and is sealed with the gift of money or property. Here the Roman client was expected to contribute money to the dowry of the patron's daughter. This is the explanation of the barely comprehensible scenes in *Godfather* from the wedding of the Don's daughter, Connie. Don Corleone's most faithful henchman, the terrifying Luca Brassi, rehearses and then enacts his duty of handing to the Don his contribution to Connie's dowry. Luca Brassi is behaving like a traditional Roman client just as the Don was behaving like a Roman patron in his dealings with Bonasera. The ancient tradition is alive and meaningful.

Books and movies both indicate that author Mario Puzo was conscious of this cultural continuity. In *Godfather*'s last scene, Michael's wife, Kay, sees the clients gather around Michael to kiss his ring in sign of obedience to the new Godfather. In the parallel scene in the novel, Michael reminds Kay of a Roman emperor. In *Godfather Part II*, Tom Hagen persuades Frank Pentangeli to commit suicide by reminding him of Roman custom and promises Frank that Michael will behave like a Roman emperor and spare Frank's family. (By this point in *Godfather Part II* Tom and Frank are the last two members loyal to the old ways on which the Corleone family was built.)

The movie's climactic scene is a *tour de force* that may never be equaled because the cinematic fireworks serve not only to arouse, but much more to educate the audience. Michael assumes his position as leader by standing as Godfather to his sister Connie's baby. At the same time his men destroy the other Mafia leaders of New York, who are gathering to assassinate him. Michael is the religious, executive, and military leader of his family, which like the Latin *familia* is an "extended family," including his natural family, their relatives, and his clients.

That the religious leader of his people should also be the commander in chief of the armed forces has seemed scandalous to some, despite René Girard's well known book linking violence and the sacred. Critics have interpreted the baptism sequence of *Godfather* as sarcastic, even blasphemous, because they do not recognize the ancient traditions it reflects. In this scene, Michael as Godfather participates in a baptism where, on the infant's behalf, he makes the traditional promises to reject the Devil and his works while his men assassinate, often brutally, his family's enemies. Viewers who are shocked by this violence and its juxtaposition with the Catholic rite of the Sacrament of Baptism are out of touch with the traditions of the West, like the old fashioned atheist professing horror over the violence and sex of the Bible. *Godfather* is like the Bible in at least one respect. It is about real life. The Bible is full of the confused and immoral as well as the coherent and heroic. It is often as hard to follow and even as boring as Joyce's *Ulysses*. If you follow it all the way to the end, however, you will see that these events occur in a context where they make sense. "Here is life *with* God. Just look at it!"

Godfather is not a documentary about a twisted criminal society. It is about real life. This point is made emphatically when Michael goes to reconcile with his old WASP girlfriend, Kay (Diane Keaton). She is shocked that he has returned to his family and its criminal activities and so has turned his back on the mainstream life his heroism in war and his intelligence had opened up to him. "Kay," he tries to explain, "my father is no different from any other powerful man—any man who is responsible for other people, like a senator or a president." "Oh Michael!" she expostulates. "Do you know how naive you sound? Senators and presidents don't have men killed." "Now who's being naive, Kay," he answers.

The ancient Roman consul was the religious, political, and military leader of his people. As head of state, he led his people in religion, politics, and war. The Godfather "is no different from any other powerful man." These three traditional traits survive in the office of President of the United States, who is commander in chief of the armed forces, presides over the executive branch, and acts as national religious leader by proclaiming every year holidays to thank God for His blessings on the nation (Thanksgiving) and to celebrate the birth of God's son, Jesus Christ (Christmas). The separation of church and state of the First Amendment to the United States Constitution was meant to protect the individual states from the national government, not to eliminate religion from the life of the young nation. Jefferson's notion of a "wall of separation" between religion and the nation's politics is one of his most disastrous lucubrations, as untrue to history as it is impossible in practice. Even the old USSR, an atheist nation, had sacred scriptures and martyrs and preserved the bodies of its saints for public veneration.

The Constitution's silence on the role of religion in the national government was soon made good by the actions and proclamations of the first President, George Washington. As John Adams noted in a letter to Dr. Benjamin Rush (June 19, 1789): "I wish with all my heart, that the Constitution had expressed as much homage to the Supreme Ruler of the Universe as the President has done in his first speech. The *Petits Maîtres* who call themselves Legislators and attempt to found a government on any other than an eternal basis of Morals and

Religion, have as much of my Pity as can consist with Contempt." Adams' comments are echoed by many statements of Washington, Jefferson, and others, which I quoted in the earlier chapter on federalism and Christianity. The judicial attempts to eliminate Christianity from the life of the United States will probably fail as an attempt to impose atheism. If they do not lead to a crisis of national morale, they will only succeed in replacing traditional Christianity with another religion, perhaps the Gnosticism analyzed by Yale Professor Harold Bloom in several recent books. There will still be a national cult, including, no doubt, a day in honor of Mother Earth. Earth, Gaia, was recognized as a divinity as early as Hesiod's *Theogony* in the seventh century B.C., although her current cult is largely a twentieth century innovation, and not the restoration of native tradition, as Sam D. Gill has shown in *Mother Earth: An American Story*.

The success of *Godfather* as a work of art is not due to the technological fireworks in which it abounds, but its moral and political maturity. Its sequel, *Godfather Part II* (ranked 32 by the AFI), weaves a complicated pattern that contrasts and mirrors the lives of two leaders. We see the young Don Corleone succeed as man and leader by following a morality of loyalty to family and friends and revenge on enemies. In the next generation, his son and successor, Michael, moves away from the moral basis on which his father's political power rested and tries to build his power on the cash nexus. He ends by losing his family and friends. Although a very powerful film, it seems to me less successful than its predecessor. Kay's abortion of Michael's second son is necessary for the plot, but seems to me out of character. Near the end Michael succeeds in killing his greatest enemy, Hyman Roth, who is shot by a hired assassin who is then himself killed. It has been made plain by this time that loyalty to Michael is based on money. Michael explains this point to Tom Hagen: "All our people are businessmen. Their loyalty is based on that." It is the central theme of the great speech that Roth (Lee Strasberg) makes to Michael in Cuba. Roth's personal and professional hero was Moe Green, the founder of Las Vegas, who was brutally and memorably killed at Michael's command during the baptismal sequence of *Godfather*. Despite his personal loyalty and affection, Roth renounces revenge to ally himself with the murderer of his friend, because he can make money if he does. "I never asked who gave the order—because this is the business we have chosen." Seen in this light, his assassination makes no sense. How can you persuade someone to go on a suicide mission for money? Only personal or family loyalty or patriotism or religion can do that. Roth's assassination is necessary for the plot. Michael needs to be completely successful in his business life while his family sinks into ruin, but the movie's premises have precluded the murder.

Another American movie that develops the theme of leadership and tradition is Disney's *The Lion King*. Most Disney films of the *fin de siècle* are not so much bad as uninteresting, their bouncy action pervaded by a treacly political correctness. *The Lion King,* however, was made at a time of political crisis at the studio, when CEO Michael Eisner was fighting to maintain control against his rival, Jeffrey Katzenberg. Eisner needed a mega hit and allowed the film's producers to make a real movie. No subsequent Disney cartoon, and there have been some relatively successful ones, has surpassed it. *The Lion King's* artistic success and enduring popularity are based on the moral and political maturity of its theme, how a young lion cub learns who he is and becomes it.

The young cub, Simba, is born to the rejoicing of the entire savannah and introduced to them in a religious ritual. (My seven year-old son leaned over to me as we watched and whispered, "That's a baptism.") Simba is raised in a world of natural hierarchy and reciprocity, in which every element and animal has its place and knows it, the Circle of Life, as his father, the King, explains to him. Simba objects that the circle is incomplete. "But, father, we eat the antelopes and no one eats us." "We die, son," his father replies, "and our bodies are buried and become grass and the antelopes eat the grass." Simba dreams of the day he will be the king of this world, a role he childishly sees as one of irresponsible power and privilege. Suddenly, in one day, his world is destroyed. His deformed and corrupt uncle, Scar, plots with the parasitic and ruthless jackals to kill the King in a way that convinces Simba that it was his fault. Overcome with guilt, Simba runs away and lives a life of harmless but frivolous horseplay in the forest with lower animals. One day by accident he meets his cousin and she tells him how the jackals, using Scar, have bled the rich life of the savannah dry. Only Simba, the natural leader, can return and restore order and prosperity.

Simba feels that he is guilty and so unworthy of the enormous responsibility to which he was born. This is a sign that he is ready to be a leader, as a future bishop must be able to say with sincerity, "*nolo episcopari.*" Then, in a scene as powerful as the one in which Michael Corleone tells his father, "I am with you now," Simba has a vision of his father. He is alive! In fact Simba is staring into a quiet pool and seeing himself. This is the supreme sign of maturity in a world where Rousseau has taught us to say, "I am no better than others, but at least I am different." Simba sees his father and understands that he is looking at himself. He is ready to overcome his guilt and assume his responsibility to restore the Circle of Life. If he allows his guilt to cause him to refuse his role, the circle will be broken. Any generation may drop the torch of tradition and plunge future ages into darkness.

We think of the leader as the ultimate individual. *Godfather* and *Lion King* show us leaders who reject individual concerns, with success in Michael's case, with guilt in Simba's, to participate in the traditions of family and society. Hollywood has made many self-indulgent and degrading films, but on occasional it makes movies that have challenged the American people. In *The Prisoner of Zenda*, Madeleine Carroll is born to be princess and wife of the heir to the throne. The man she loves, Ronald Colman, has saved her country from its selfish enemies, and now he asks her to go off with him because they love one another. Her duty, however, is to marry the king, whom she does not love. "I don't know why God let me fall in love with you," she tells Colman, but she must follow tradition and do her duty. In *Terminator*, directed by James Cameron from a script written by himself and Gale Anne Hurd, Linda Hamilton plays an ordinary American girl, not especially smart or chaste, who achieves human fulfillment. She does this not by mastering the male arts of violence and power, like the heroines of *Network* and *Alien*, but by learning that she is a woman and a mother and becoming what she was born to be. In *Terminator*'s climactic scene she makes love to Michael Biehn, with whom she has struggled and learned, in the full consciousness that they are begetting the future leader of their race. She has grown from a moral adolescent who cares only for the next date to a woman who can take responsibility for her future child and the next generation.

Most Hollywood movies do not teach lessons of loyalty to the past and responsibility for the future. Fifteen years after *Terminator* James Cameron made the most successful movie of the twentieth century (reckoned in inflated dollars). The most expensive and most innovative technology ever devoted to a movie went into the making of *Titanic,* about the unsinkable ocean liner whose catastrophic collision with an iceberg showed, or tried to show, the twentieth century how unsafe it is for erring human beings to rely on technology. The heroine, played by Kate Winslet, is a bright young woman returning to America on the *Titanic* to enter into a loveless marriage which will save her family from financial ruin and social scandal. The lower decks are crowded with people fleeing poverty and Europe for the New World. The upper decks house *soi-disant* aristocrats, who are only *nouveaux riches* plutocrats. In an act of rebellion against the loveless fate to which her father's selfishness has condemned her, Winslet makes love to one of the poor Americans, Leonardo DiCaprio. With his help, she survives the wreck and returns at the end of the century (as Gloria Stewart) to tell a group of technologically advanced but morally obtuse treasure hunters that her brief liaison "saved me in every sense in which a person can be saved."

Aristotle thought that "To live according to your country's way of life is not slavery. It is salvation." Cameron, obviously, was not thinking of that definition of salvation any more than he was of the Christian sense. (If he was thinking of the Christian sense, it was to repudiate it.) At the end of *Terminator,* Linda Hamilton tells her unborn child that in the short time she and the baby's father spent together, they loved enough for a lifetime. Their relationship involved not only their brief time together in a motel, but also a future where the child that is the fruit of their fertile lovemaking will grow up to lead and save his people from a terrible foe. The brief hour the heroine of *Titanic* spent with the hero also changed her life. The sterile act enjoyed by the healthy Winslet and the skinny DiCaprio frees Winslet to be a true modern individual, without fiancé, family, religion, or any other obligation except that of self-fulfillment. She is the female equivalent of Jack Nicholson's character in *Carnal Knowledge*. DiCaprio has taught her "to be a survivor." In *Terminator* Michael Biehn gives his life so that his child and his people can survive in the future. In *Titanic* Leonardo DiCaprio dies so that his partner in a brief liaison can desert family and social station to seek a life of self-fulfillment. *Vita gratia vitae*, "life for life's sake."

Titanic's *dénouement* possesses bittersweet pathos, but no tragedy. Tragedy as an emotion and a genre is foreign to Hollywood, since it depends on moral conflict and not technological display. Movies that possess tragic conflict are often not very successful as works of art: *The Green Berets* or *Walking Tall*. Their themes are Roman and not Greek. Aeneas loses his family so that he can lead his people to a new home. This story pattern is rarely found in artistically successful movies. Exceptions include some of John Ford's Westerns. The AFI list included the socialist pathos of *Grapes of Wrath* (21) and the naive individualism of

Stagecoach (63), but found no room for *She Wore A Yellow Ribbon* or *The Man Who Shot Liberty Valance*, although *The Searchers* managed to squeeze in at number 96. In the last three movies John Wayne plays men who sacrifice home and family to fight barbarism and violence so that other Americans can live in an ordered and peaceful society. Behind the main plot, we glimpse irreplaceable loss: a family massacred, brave men dying without children, the defeat of the Confederacy.

Against the *leitmotiv* of a new society built on loss and sacrifice, there plays in ironic counterpoint the theme of the illusions which the peaceful society maintains to hide from itself the sacrifices which were needed for its foundation. At the end of *The Man Who Shot Liberty Valance*, the aggressive newspaperman who was so hungry for a story at the movie's opening discovers that the violent gunslinger Liberty Valance was not killed by Jimmy Stewart, the soft-spoken Eastern lawyer who rode to political success because people believed he shot Valance in a duel. No, the man who really shot Liberty Valance was John Wayne, whose reward was to die without fame or heir. The newsman decides that his professional duty is to legend, not to truth, and suppresses the story. The scene recalls Ford's *Fort Apache*, where at the end Wayne allows the reputation of the bigoted martinet, Henry Fonda (in Fonda's finest performance), to remain unbesmirched by the complicated and uninspiring truth. The new country needs heroes more than it needs truth. The most famous image from a John Ford movie is the last shot in *Searchers* where John Wayne walks away from the family and society he has reunited at terrible cost to himself. Like the leftist ideologue of Steinbeck's *Viva Zapata!*, he has no country or farm, no family or wife. He did not cast them away because he was driven by lust for power. He sacrificed his chance for them to do his duty. The Hollywood Happy Ending is for other people.

Two places below *The Searchers* on the AFI list was Clint Eastwood's *Unforgiven*. It was the only one of his very successful movies to make the list. (No movie directed by Don Siegel made the list, not *Dirty Harry* or *Invasion of the Body Snatchers* or *Madigan*.) As often with the AFI list, ideology was the key factor. Eastwood allowed *Unforgiven* to be marketed as a repudiation of the violent movies which helped make him one of the pop icons of the generation that began watching him in the early 60s in *Rawhide* on television and then in the movies that began with Sergio Leone's spaghetti westerns and culminated in his most famous part, *Dirty Harry*.

Recent discussions have rejected the idea of *Unforgiven* as a Stesichorean palinode sung by Eastwood to demonstrate repentance for his earlier successes. The movie ends with the dedication "To Sergio and Don." Would Eastwood dedicate to the two best directors he ever worked with, men whose work lies at the foundation of his own career, a movie which rejected their greatest films? I cannot believe that. *Unforgiven* possesses several traits that appealed to Hollywood: it was interpreted as a deconstruction of Eastwood's popular movies and is replete with horrendous violence and a pervasive verbal obscenity. It appears on the AFI's list as a backhanded acknowledgment of Eastwood's importance, just as the Academy of Motion Picture Arts and Sciences systematically ignored John Wayne's best work and gave him an Academy Award for a silly performance in a bad movie, 1969's *True Grit.* That is no reason for us to be taken in.

Unforgiven differs from other Eastwood action movies because his usual Roman themes of loss and sacrifice are elided in favor of Greek themes of human limitation and tragic error. As in *Dirty Harry* the conflict is between a savage killer and the honest lawman who must use violence to repel violence and save society for the law-abiding citizen. In *Unforgiven,* however, the notorious killer is played by Eastwood himself, and most of the movie is seen from his point of view. It is as though *Dirty Harry* were filmed from the perspective of Andy Robinson's Scorpio Killer, instead of Eastwood's Harry Callaghan.

The Marshal of the small frontier town of Big Whiskey is Little Bill (Gene Hackman). He is trying and failing to build a home for himself and to make the town safe for decent folk. He is honest and fair, but rough. When a whore is scarred in a cathouse brawl, he arranges for what he considers fair payment.

The prostitutes are not satisfied. They want revenge in blood and offer a large reward for anyone who kills the men who scarred their friend. They are not the innocent women at the mercy of a serial killer whom we find in many Eastwood movies. They are the Furies of Aeschylus' *Eumenides*, contemptuous of compromise, interested only in a remorseless *lex talionis* of blood for blood. They spread a story of an innocent girl mutilated and offer an enormous reward. It is Hackman's job to stop their ruthless lust for revenge. When a feared English gunfighter, the Duke of Death, (played by Richard Harris) arrives in Big Whiskey, Hackman attacks him before he has a chance to act. Little Bill disarms and brutalizes the dangerous killer and then sends his broken body out of town as the women watch in impotent frustration. Then Eastwood shows up and again Little Bill beats him to within an inch of his life. Hackman is as brutally effective in the old West as Dirty Harry is in San Francisco.

Eastwood's William Munny is a more complicated character than Andy Robinson's Scorpio Killer. Munny stopped killing for pay under the influence of a good woman. His wife, however, died, a constant motif in Eastwood's movies. Left alone he is a failure as a pig farmer and, when invited by a violent young man to return one more time to his old life, he decides to go along, even though, as he says over and over, "I ain't like that no more." He calls upon his old sidekick, Ned

(Morgan Freeman), to help him. Marriage and farming have also domesticated Ned, who eventually leaves Munny and his young friend before their cruel and humiliating murder of the two cowboys the whores have targeted for death.

Although Ned left before the killings and accepted no money, Little Bill captures him. After Ned dies under Little Bill's brutal interrogation, his corpse is displayed in the window of the bar where the whore house is located. When Munny hears of his friend's death, he begins drinking again and goes looking for revenge, like Achilles seeking revenge for his best friend, Patroclus. The scene of vengeance, however, comes from Book Twenty-two of the *Odyssey*. In the *Iliad* the two great rivals face one another in single combat: Hector, the defender of his home, against Achilles, who once sought glory and now seeks only revenge. In *Unforgiven* Munny walks into the crowded bar alone, as Odysseus appears before the reveling suitors. Odysseus kills Antinous, the chief of the suitors, who is not expecting a fight and is caught off guard while drinking. The other suitors denounce the man they think is a clumsy beggar. Odysseus announces his true identity and begins to slaughter them. They are unarmed, although eventually some of them lay hands on weapons. By the end all are slain except for the bard, who will sing to future generations of Odysseus' great feat.

So Eastwood's William Munny walks into the bar and asks for the barkeep who hung his friend up for public mockery. He then shoots him dead on the spot. Little Bill responds with disgust. "You dirty coward! You shot an unarmed man." "Well, he should have armed himself, if he is going to decorate his saloon with my friend" says the impassive Eastwood and begins killing the denizens of the bar. Soon all who have not run away are dead except for a cowardly writer of westerns and the wounded Little Bill. As Eastwood stands over him, Hackman protests, "I don't deserve this—to die like this. I was building a house." Munny replies, "Deserve's got nothing to do with it." The downed epic hero, Patroclus before Hector or Hector before Achilles, predicts the death of his victorious foe. Ned had told Little Bill that Munny would come for him, as he did, and now Little Bill screams, "I'll see you in Hell, William Munny!" Eastwood grunts a derisive "Yeah!" and shoots Hackman at point blank range. The nearly hysterical writer questions the victorious Munny on his strategy. There was none. Munny killed in berserker rage. The writer determines to tell a story that will satisfy his customers, like the newspaperman in *Liberty Valance*. After taking another drink, Eastwood threatens the town if they do not bury his friend and rides away. The demoralized town is too terrified to shoot at him. At the end of the movie, we hear a rumor that Munny has left farming and moved his family to San Francisco, where he runs a successful dry goods store. His wife's mother comes to visit her daughter's grave but cannot understand why a good woman would marry such a violent man. The credits roll by, ending with the dedication to Sergio Leone and Don Siegel.

Unforgiven is about more than William Munny and the meaningless violence that punctuates his life. It is also the tragic tale of Little Bill, who did his job to create order in a world of violent men and woman and then, in one moment of frustration and rage, went too far and killed an innocent man. Tacitus noted near the start of his *Histories*, "The Gods care more for our punishment than for our reward." In the remorseless world we live in, the criminal is always allowed another chance. The good guy must not make a mistake. When Gene Hackman's Little Bill killed Morgan Freeman's Ned, he reenacted the end of the movie for which he won his first Oscar, *The French Connection*. There, after successfully frustrating violence and drug dealers, Hackman's Popeye Doyle goes too far and kills a fellow officer, while the criminal mastermind he was hunting escapes. Tragedy, as Aristotle saw it, is the story not of the success of the good or the punishment of the bad, but of the fate that meets the good man who makes a mistake (*hamartia*). In the end it is not the two murdered cowboys who are the unforgiven of the title, but Little Bill.

In Clint Eastwood's *Unforgiven* the American movie achieves tragedy. In the typical Hollywood movie the good are rewarded and the evil punished. "That's what we mean by fiction," as Oscar Wilde noted. It is also why men think they act, as Little

Bill's angry protest, "I don't deserve this," shows. After the brutal murder of the two cowboys, Eastwood's youthful accomplice tries to console himself, "Well, I guess they had it coming." "Kid," Munny replies, "we all got it coming," just as he tells Little Bill, "Deserve's got nothing to do with it." Fate obeys its own inexorable laws and the efforts of critics to discover Oedipus' tragic flaw are as futile as the moralizing of Job's friends. Newspapers and most movies exist to hide this bleak but clear-sighted vision from our eyes. The Enlightenment Project believes that social justice can trump fate. The classics teach the opposite. Whatever will turn out to work for a society, only the latter has provided the basis for much great art.

It is, I suppose, a logical possibility that meaningful art could be created on a foundation other than the genres and story patterns inherited from the classical past. We have been trying to do so for some time. Even building on that legacy is no guarantee of success. Certainly few in the entertainment industry want to hear that true creativity can come only after a long discipline of learning old and complex traditions and subjecting those traditions to critical reflection. Even then the intellectual challenge must be restrained by a moral discipline of humility before past accomplishment, of scorn for short term sensual pleasure, and of admiration for those who subordinate self to create a larger good for their society: George Bailey's Savings and Loan in *It's a Wonderful Life*, the barn-building of

Witness, the *Lion King*'s Circle of Life. *Ars gratia artis, vel potius gratia pecuniae.* We have tried art for art's sake and for money's sake. Only creating within the tradition can teach us to subordinate those necessary aspects of life—artistry and money—to the wider perspectives, to the moral and intellectual disciplines which have given us the great art we need from the past. With such perspective and discipline, we can still on occasion produce works of creative genius. Indeed, it is the best hope for its creation in the future.

Epilogue

OPTATIVES AND IMPERATIVES FOR THE NEXT MILLENNIUM

As an American, I have a grudging admiration for the Connecticut Yankee who is not satisfied with contemplating the human situation and sets about fixing the problems that can be fixed. So I shall end with suggestions, which some may view as practical:

I. Simplify the elementary school curriculum to concentrate on language and mathematics.

Grades 1-5: Language Arts (English and Latin), Math, and History/Geography. Grades 6-8: Language Arts (English and Latin), Math, History/Geography, and a Modern Language.

A glance at the schedule of a good elementary school shows that the school week is chopped up into too many subjects presented too superficially. These defects are present even in such fine curricula as those worked out by E. D. Hirsch, Jr., and his associates. The truth is that teachers are overworked and students are under-prepared in a wide spectrum of areas. We need to limit the number of subjects taught and increase what is learned. Students will be prepared to explore different areas in college, instead of taking what are in effect remedial courses.

An elementary school curriculum emphasizing language and mathematics, with a strong grounding in Greek myth and Roman political institutions, would prepare students to read great and challenging works of literature, to use the language of serious discourse, and to understand the republican tradition. Strong preparation in mathematics helps students advance rapidly in science when they reach high school and university. When Jefferson said, "If a nation expects to be ignorant and free, in a state of civilization, it expects what never was and never will be," he was thinking about this kind of curriculum, as we see in his *Notes on the State of Virginia*.

Elementary school is the time to study subjects that are important for learning other disciplines. Latin is basic in this sense. As John Stuart Mill pointed out, someone who knows Latin can learn all the romance languages more easily than a Latin-less student can learn any one of them. Greek myth provides the themes of Western art and permeates the language and thought of great writers. Shakespeare really is not comprehensible to someone who does not know the myths of the Greeks. Neither is Milton. Neither is T. S. Eliot.

An elementary school curriculum that emphasizes ancient languages and mathematics may seem like another burden on the shoulders of America's overworked teachers. There are, however, excellent programs for teaching basic Latin in elementary school that actually render the process fun. Teachers have to be bright and interested, but they do not need to be experts in Latin. "Language Arts through Latin," developed in Philadelphia under the leadership of Rudolph Masciantonio and William Torchia, is easy to teach and exciting for both students and teachers. Developed to fit into the language arts curriculum of the normal elementary school, it has been successfully modified to fit the needs of students in other urban areas, such as Los Angeles and Indianapolis. The intellectual challenge of the subjects makes teaching them exciting. (Masciantonio promotes his program as a cure for teacher burnout.) Language Arts through Latin and more mathematics can be introduced into American elementary schools without placing heavy demands on the current faculty. In fact, moving from a supermarket model offering many disparate subjects to concentrating on fewer subjects taught more intensively would reduce preparation time. Of course, concentration means eliminating some subjects, but the long-term gains will outweigh the short-term losses. What students learn in elementary school about mathematics and foreign languages is the students' for life; what they learn about science will be obsolete before they get to college.

In the most creative periods of the past millennium, including the Renaissance, the Reformation, and most of American history, students in grammar schools studied Greek, Latin, and mathematics. As recently as the early 1960s there were more than 700,000 Latin students in American high schools. The high schools of Virginia still provide models of successful Latin programs, and many home schoolers teach their children Latin. This is a reform that has worked in the past and still works when given a chance.

II. Take teacher certification away from the schools of education.

Many thoughtful proposals for improving the quality of teaching exist, but the cheapest and the best would be to drop current certification requirements. Education schools want future teachers to learn how to teach by taking education courses. We do not teach figure skating by handing future Olympic hopefuls a textbook on skating, subjecting them to a course of lectures, and then, after they have passed a few written exams, sending them out to compete. New skaters first become the disciples of master skaters. Observation of a master, countless practice sessions, regular criticism, and much guidance constitute the traditional route to acquiring new skills. In fact, it is the only route, and it is also the way to learn teaching.

To improve teaching, states should establish a training program built around Master Teachers, who, because of their superior teaching skills, would spend part of their time training other teachers. Teaching schools with Master Teachers could operate in much the same way as teaching hospitals do. We might want to require future teachers to graduate from college with a reading mastery of Latin, along with advanced oral proficiency in a Romance language. There should also be a solid mathematics requirement and a high GPA cutoff. If we really want A teachers, we should not accept B and C undergraduate students. This method will produce fewer teachers than the current system. But we would have several hundred teachers who could teach well, instead of thousands of teachers making it through class cribbing from the teachers' editions of the textbooks they are assigned to teach.

There are several advantages to this scheme. Over the period of a generation the quality of elementary and high school teachers would rise. Most people get into teaching in order to teach, but over time they get discouraged at the amount of baby-sitting and administrative duties involved. A curriculum that concentrates on teaching a small number of challenging topics—topics that relate to many other subjects—will attract people who want to teach and give them reasons to stay.

Furthermore, there will never be a time when all positions in society are filled with the wise and the beautiful, but we can at least keep the worst out. This is the point of government inspection of meat. No program can guarantee that all food is of the highest quality. Quality control is there to protect us from dying of diseased and contaminated food.

Certification, like government inspection of meat, was intended to ensure a certain level of teaching, but certification has had almost the opposite effect because it is controlled by the education schools, which historically have been committed to downplaying a teacher's acquisition of knowledge of a subject in favor of his memorizing textbook methodology. Richard Morin in the *Washington Post* (November 17, 1997) reported a survey taken by Public Agenda of 900 education professors, which concluded, "Professors of education hold a vision of public education that seems fundamentally at odds with that of the public school teachers, students, and the public." For instance, only 19 percent of professors surveyed said it was important for teachers "to stress correct spelling, grammar and punctuation in their teaching." Only 57 percent of those surveyed felt it was "absolutely necessary" for teachers to be "deeply knowledgeable about the content of the specific subjects they will be teaching." Should we be surprised if "somewhat knowledgeable" teachers produce ignorant pupils?

George Lyon in the *Phi Delta Kappan* (October 1984) summarized the indictment and the remedy: "The monopoly of the education schools must be broken; there must be other paths to certification. Since teaching is a pragmatic art best learned by experience, school districts should establish apprenticeship programs for people who can satisfy literacy requirements and show a command of subject matter." Most states now test future teachers in basics. The most popular tests are the Praxis series, developed by the Educational Testing Service, and now used by 35 states. In February, 1998, Virginia governor James S. Gilmore announced that one-third of future teachers in Virginia had failed Praxis I, which tests reading, writing, and mathematics. Virginia has the nation's highest cutoff score for Praxis I. Barely half of the students in the other 19 states which use Praxis I would have passed at Virginia's level. Testing teachers is a useful tool, but it is not enough.

III. America's churches should start teaching the Sacred Tongues.

Our contact with the traditions we need to survive and prosper cannot be left in the hands of professional educators. The institutions which most clearly need and maintain contact with the past are the Christian churches of America. They have inherited and continue to maintain a massive system of Sunday schools, Bible reading programs, Vacation Bible schools, preschools, traditional elementary schools, high schools, colleges, universities, and seminaries, but in this vast system there is little time devoted to teaching and learning the Sacred Tongues. By the time the pious future preacher enters seminary, it is usually too late to learn much Greek, Hebrew, Latin, and German. Meanwhile, the parishioner is confused by a plethora of different translations. The time to begin is in Sunday school, at the pre-school and elementary level. There are a number of programs for teaching Latin at that level, and the field is wide open for developing Greek and Hebrew programs. As any parent will tell you, it is not hard to get children to learn the alphabet and increase their vocabularies at an elementary level. Children learn words with ease, and the foundation for a lifelong familiarity with the Scriptures could begin in childhood.

Congregations rarely think about the potential for spiritual and intellectual growth in this area. Many churches, seeing their attendance slipping, have founded preschools to reach out to their communities in a way that is consistent with Christian tradition. And yet these programs, which do so much to protect and nurture children, could do so much more in the way of cultural education than they do currently. These programs could give children nothing less than an introduction to the mental infrastructure of their religious and secular traditions. It is a great blessing that Plato and Aristotle wrote in the same language as Paul and John, and that Virgil and Augustine, Cicero and Aquinas share a common tongue. Now, I would myself encourage the use of the King James translation for liturgical purposes, but no translation can replace the original text for study and meditation. These are the words of eternal life. When John Paul II was leading his enormously successful youth rally in Denver, he asked at one point for the assembled congregation to join him in the

Lord's Prayer "in Latino." Not many under forty joined in. That rare false note in an exciting event was a significant moment, and it illustrates my point perfectly. We are cutting our children off from their traditions.

These few suggestions constitute this book's optatives. The optative is the Greek mood of wishing. What, then, are its imperatives, the things we must do? The imperative of this book is the return to tradition, the Great Tradition with which we must never lose touch and the little traditions we love and are meant to love, though in the end we shall see them disappear, like the old Episcopalian Prayer Book, celebrating Washington's birthday, or wishing one another a "Merry Christmas." In our age "it is only the inconsistency we live off of that has kept us from silencing every tradition," as Gerhard Krüger put it. That inconsistency, however, is rooted in healthy instincts. "We are called to be disciples, not energumens," wrote Albert Jay Nock. "The Great Tradition will go on because the forces of nature are on its side." It is the element in which we live and prosper and create.

Few of us are chosen to be leaders, but all of us are chosen, at some point in our lives, to perform certain acts and say certain words. The words will usually be ones we ourselves have not composed. At the end of *Play it Again, Sam*, Woody Allen's Allan Felix goes to the airport with Diane Keaton, as she thinks, to tell Tony Roberts that she is leaving him. Instead Woody tells her to get on the plane with her husband. He explains, "You are part of his work, the thing that keeps him going. If that plane leaves the ground and you're not with him, you'll regret it. Maybe not today, maybe not tomorrow, but soon and for the rest of your life." Flabbergasted, Keaton says, "That's the most beautiful thing I ever heard" and Woody answers, "It's from *Casablanca*. I've been waiting my whole life to say it."

Audiences always howl with laughter at that scene, but it has a serious message. Even in a comic vision of the world, the truly moral act comes not from a spontaneous movement of an untutored soul or an impulse from a vernal wood but from having memorized the words and saying them at the right time. Few of us will ever be leaders, but we can still be Allan Felix. We just have to know our part.

When our cue comes, may we know our lines and say them clearly.

Appendix

DOING IT ON YOUR OWN

A famous squib in the English comic magazine, *Punch,* runs: "Advice to those about to marry: Don't."

I won't repeat that advice to those interested in studying Greek or Latin on their own, but it is difficult work. The old farmer in Eugene O'Neill's *Desire Under the Elms* (a tragedy modeled on Euripides' *Hippolytus*) repeats over and over again the basis of his theology: "God ain't easy. God's hard." So are Greek and Latin.

The best time to begin language study (and the study of mathematics) is before puberty, as Thomas Jefferson knew and contemporary research has confirmed. The best way is in a class with other interested learners under the direction of a committed teacher. Getting a decent instructor might seem difficult, but many Americans live near colleges and universities where these languages are taught. Most priests and ministers are interested in

Greek and Latin as well, so a good way to review the languages is to organize a class for interested parishioners. Again, learning languages is difficult for adults; it takes time and concentration and often develops slowly. But just when it seems that you are going nowhere, all of a sudden, you find yourself on a higher plateau.

Excellent introductions for the loner have just been published, *Learn Latin* (Barnes and Noble) and *Learn Ancient Greek* (Duckworth), by English Classicist Peter Jones. Both books are lively and entertaining and introduce the reader to enough grammar and vocabulary to read bits of the Bible and other prose and poetry, though Jones does not give a complete course. (He leaves out the future tense, for instance.) The student is meant to work through a chapter per week, but even if you take out a few weeks to give yourself a breather, you will get through either book in less than six months. In fact, near the beginning of the third month of *Learn Latin*, you will be reading bits of the Bible and singing "Oh Come All Ye Faithful" in Latin: "*Adeste Fideles.*" By the middle of the fourth month, you are reading Catullus' "*odi et amo.*" There are only two lines in this poem by Catullus, but after you read them you will be hooked on Latin. It is a long way from there to Cicero and Virgil, to Augustine and Aquinas, and a very long way to Tacitus, but by the time you get to Catullus you will already know much about Latin vocabulary, culture, and literature.

Once you have mastered Jones, there are many ways to go on beyond him. If you have a teacher, use the book your teacher is comfortable with. I have seen good teachers work wonders with the most intractable texts. The traditional Latin text which possesses the most help in the same volume and for which various other supplementary material is available is Frederick M. Wheelock, *Latin: An Introductory Course*, Fifth Edition, by Richard LaFleur. (Centaur Systems has software packets to review grammar, vocabulary, and translation.) Latin courses that teach grammar through reading connected passages include Peter V. Jones and Keith Sidwell, *Reading Latin* (Cambridge) and Maurice Balme and James Morwood, *Oxford Latin Course*. These books are meant for adults. Many, however, will prefer high school Latin courses, such as the *Cambridge Latin Course* and the Scottish *Ecce Romani!* (The latter is available in an American edition from Scott-Foresman by Gilbert Lawall *et al.*) Other readers will want to wander down to the local used book store and pick up an older text, like B. L. Ullman's *Latin for Americans* or Charles Jenney's *First Year Latin*. But once you have worked through Peter Jones's *Learn Latin* you will be well on your way to a profitable use of any of these texts.

One place to get younger children started is with *Salvete! A First Course in Latin*. This book is lively and leads into the *Cambridge Latin Course*, but the chapters are not consistent in presenting material; and elementary school kids prefer less daily life and more myth, in my experience. Another good textbook at this level is Marion Polsky's *First Latin* (Scott-Foresman). *How the Romans Lived and Spoke* was designed as a Teachers' Guide for an oral/aural introduction to Latin for fifth graders in the Philadelphia School District. It can be successful as early as the third grade. Although used in many urban school districts over the past twenty years, *How the Romans Lived and Spoke* is not easily available to the ordinary citizen, so you will have to hunt. For absolute beginners, I recommend *Learning Latin Through Mythology* (Cambridge), which is fun and has vocabulary that stays with them. Once beginners have worked through some grammar, you might want to try the Greek myths in *Fabulae Graecae* (Scott-Foresman), a revision of a successful old reader, traditionally known as *Ritchie's Fabulae Faciles*. The revision gives a lot of help to teacher and student.

Before your Latin is in any condition to allow you access to its classical texts, you will want to try out various authors in translation. The Penguin and Oxford World Classics are rich in interesting texts translated into a lively and readable English. But don't forget to check out your used book store. The key is to select the translation which fits your taste. Latin literature is rich in history. Most people will prefer to start with Suetonius' juicy stories of the *Lives of the Twelve Caesars* before moving on to Tacitus' more political and more cynical *Annals* and *Histories*, or Livy's tales of the early Republic and the great war with

Hannibal of Carthage. Sallust's *Jugurthine War* and *Conspiracy of Catiline*, brief vignettes of two crises of the late Roman Republic, are lively and influenced the American Founders. You might be interested to learn from Cato's speech that pagan Romans thought people who betrayed their country suffered in the Underworld after they died.

There are a number of good translations of Virgil's *Aeneid* available, including the verse translations of Allen Mandelbaum, Robert Fitzgerald, and C. Day Lewis (the actor's father). John Dryden's version is available in an inexpensive paperback. It is very important for the history of English verse, but may be heavy going for most readers. The Penguin prose versions of Jackson Knight and David West are both lively. West's is more accurate, despite the fact that Jackson Knight contacted Virgil through a medium to help him with some problems. Most of the myths we remember come from Ovid's *Metamorphoses*. My experience is that children prefer myths to history and the details of daily life that interest Latin textbook writers. *Learning Latin through Mythology* is straight out of Ovid.

All the textbooks I have mentioned get the user into reading Latin authors relatively rapidly, but non-classical and Christian Latin tends to be slighted. Your local Christian bookstore, however, may have the New Testament in Latin; if not, have them order it from the American Bible Society. If you are really ambitious, ask them to get hold of St. Jerome's translation of the entire Bible, which is known as the Vulgate. For other non-classical authors, you may need to go to a university library and Xerox. That is the easiest way to get hold of Luther's *De libertate christiana*. The same is true of Thomas Aquinas, although copies of the *Summa Theologica* show up now and then in used book stores or on the Internet. Theologians always plug his difficult theological arguments, but much of the Second Part of the *Summa Theologica* is devoted to moral issues, which are more easily apprehended. Still, it is hard to find your way around at first, because the Second Part is divided into two parts, *Prima Secundae* and *Secunda Secundae*. If you are working with a class, or even on your own, you might find it fun to work through the Latin of the Second Article of the Sixty-fourth Question of the *Secunda Secundae*. The subject is the Death Penalty, and the issues raised are still with us. If you hear your parish priest or local bishop discuss the Death Penalty, you can ask if he agrees with Saint Thomas. Some will be pleased and excited you asked.

There are many good ways to get Latin. But the same is not true for Greek. Fortunately Peter Jones's *Learn Ancient Greek* complements his *Learn Latin*. With this book too the student ends up reading the Bible and some good poetry. For New Testament Greek at a more difficult level, there is the fine theological conservative J. Gresham Machen's *Introduction to New Testament Greek*. The best traditional textbook is Crosby and Schaeffer, *An Introduction to Greek*, written in the 1920s for high school students and still in print as late the 1960s. (They review the imperative by giving the student the Lord's Prayer in Greek from Matthew.) If you find a copy in your local used book store, snap it up. For classical Greek there is Chase and Phillips, *Introduction to Greek*. All these texts were meant to be worked through in a school year; and you will need to take time with Greek, so be patient with yourself.

Parallel to the Latin series from Cambridge and Oxford are *Reading Greek* (Cambridge) and *Athenaze* (Oxford). Donald J. Mastronarde's *Introduction to Attic Greek* (Berkeley) has a useful *Electronic Workbook* for MacIntosh. Once you have worked through these texts, which will be easier if you have done Jones first, there are good supplementary volumes with reading material from Cambridge. *The Intellectual Revolution* has exciting passages from Thucydides and Plato, including parts of Socrates' *Apology*, some of which you will have already read if you used *Reading Greek*. A *World of Heroes* contains some wonderful passages from Homer's *Iliad* and Sophocles' *Oedipus the King*.

The language of the New Testament is Greek. Your local Christian bookstore can get you *The Greek New Testament* (United Bible Societies) with a vocabulary in the back. Every week prepare the *pericopes*—the epistle and Gospel readings in Church. It will be hard going at first, and some parts of Paul never get any easier, but eventually you will find the Gospel stories readable and even fun. And not all of Paul is heavy going. Galatians is quite straightforward with some very clear narrative. Unfortunately few churches read the beginning of the fifth chapter when he finally loses his temper with the circumcision crowd. And no translation quite gives the effect verse 12 has in the original Greek.

While you are learning Greek, you will also want to read the Greek authors in translation. Everybody does. English translations of the classics constitute a bull market in the publishing trade. Let's start with Homer, perhaps the most famous Greek poet. Are you a Robert Fitzgerald person, an Allen Mandelbaum person, a Richmond Lattimore person or a Robert Fagles person? Or do you prefer Lattimore's *Iliad* but Fitzgerald's *Odyssey*? (Me? Ignore me. I am for Alexander Pope's rendition of Homer, but John Keats was not wrong to be swept away by Chapman's Homer.) If you go hunting in used book stores, you can find the prose version done a century ago by Andrew Lang and his associates. This version is the most accurate one I know, but people object that it sounds like the King James Bible. Personally I like the King James Version, so follow your own taste.

When you have read Homer, you are in the situation Adam and Eve find themselves at the end of *Paradise Lost*:

The world was all before them, where to choose
Their place of rest, and Providence their guide.

I suggest you start with the Greek historians. Herodotus' account of the ancient Near East, which culminates in the great story of the Persian Empire's attempt to conquer Greece, has become something of a best-seller again because of the popularity of the movie *The English Patient*. Thucydides' narrative of the war between Athens and Sparta is a picture of democracy in action which is ever relevant to Americans. Moreover, Polybius' description of the Roman Republic in Book VI of his *Universal History* helped shape the United States. (The Penguin is called *The Rise of the Roman Empire*.) If you like Suetonius and are trying to find a Greek parallel, try Procopius' *Secret History*. It is the inside gossip of the court of the Christian monarch Justinian and his queen Theodora during the sixth century A.D., a thousand years after Herodotus and Thucydides.

The world of Greek tragedy is one so rich that I am tempted to say—just wander. Some people will prefer Aeschylus. Once you have a year or two of Greek under your belt, you will find his *Prometheus* quite readable. It was Karl Marx's favorite Greek tragedy. *The Persians* is a patriotic play on the Persian attempt to conquer Greece in which the tragic hero is the enemy. Imagine Hollywood in the late forties producing *Das Boot*. The *Oresteia* is a trilogy about men and women, revenge and justice, divine kingship and human democracy, and I am leaving out a lot. It was the *Oresteia* which inspired Richard Wagner to take some very unimpressive German myths and turn them into his magnificent

Nibelung's Ring. The first play, *Agamemnon*, may be the greatest Greek tragedy and is one of the hardest to read in Greek.

Aristotle's favorite Greek tragedy was Sophocles' *Oedipus*. It is the one Greek myth almost everyone knows. What Freud did with this play and its story is one of the great examples of the creativity that comes from returning to the origins of Western culture—and demonstrates to my satisfaction that even the opponents of tradition need to return to the traditions. Hegel's favorite tragedy was Sophocles' *Antigone*, a play as rich as the *Oresteia*, but much more focused. In one famous speech, Antigone gives the rationale for civil disobedience used by everybody from Socrates to M. L. King. Yet the play is not really about that, or, perhaps better, is about much more than that.

I have already suggested too many plays and we have not yet gotten to Euripides: the burning hot passion of *Medea*; the ice cold but still burning classical perfection of *Hippolytus*; the pageant-like *Trojan Women*. But above all, there is the *Bacchae*. It is the Greek tragedy that has held the most appeal to people in the twentieth century, though the drama seems to mean something different to each producer and translator and reader. It was Gilbert Murray's translation in 1903 that inspired Shaw's *Major Barbara*. In 1998 Mark David Epstein's version capped the recent Penn Greek Drama Series. And yet William Arrowsmith's translation (1959) in the University of Chicago *Complete Greek Tragedies* series remains simple and powerful.

When you have studied Greek for a few years, try the *Bacchae*. The language is challenging, but when the tragic hero faces his end, there is a line so simple that everyone who knows even a little Greek can translate it, and so powerful that no one who has read it has ever forgotten it.

In addition to all this there is Greek philosophy. For many readers, the book that will stay with them was written not by a classical Greek, but by a Roman emperor in the second century A.D. Marcus Aurelius' *Meditations* still speaks to us, as we strive to maintain our humanity in a world which seems out of control. The Stoics will always have an audience and, of all of them, this Roman emperor remains the most accessible.

Of the famous Greek philosophers of the fourth century A.D., Aristotle is the hardest. His *Nicomachean Ethics* is full of wisdom, and thought provoking. His lectures on *Politics* are challenging, and perhaps even more thought provoking. The rest of his work, including his very important research into science, is hard to read on your own. G. E. R. Lloyd's *Aristotle: The Growth and Structure of his Thought* (1968) is the book that has helped me the most, but there are a number of other good introductions.

Ultimately, however, we read Greek to meet two people: Jesus and Socrates. Neither wrote anything that has survived. They are quoted and written about by very different types of people. Those people are interesting in their own right, and scholars like to write about the differences between Matthew and John, for instance, or Plato and Xenophon. That work is for later. In the beginning, we want to know about Jesus and Socrates. For Jesus we have the four Gospels. For Socrates we have Plato, Xenophon, and Aristophanes.

You want to start with Plato: *Socrates' Apology* (his defense speech before the Athenian jury) and the dialogue *Crito*, in which Socrates tries to explain to a loving old friend why he is going to accept the jury's unjust verdict and die. (By the way, except for the first page or two of the *Apology*, both works are fairly easy to read in the original. *Reading Greek* has you working through part of the *Apology* during your first year.) Socrates is to Greek what "*odi et amo*" is to Latin. Once you meet him, you want more.

And there is much more. I do not know what to advise you to read next from Plato's large corpus of dialogues; there is something there for everybody. The obvious next step is *Phaedo*, the dialogue where Socrates' death is described and we are introduced to "Plato's Theory of Ideas." (They are not "ideas" in our sense, and it is not a "theory." Moreover, the "theory " may well be Plato's, but not if you asked Plato, who always attributed it to his teacher Socrates.) The *Phaedo* gives us the high tragedy of the philosophic life—and the comic side of that life is the *Symposium*. In this dialogue, Socrates goes to a drinking party, where the guests send the dancing girls away and start delivering a series of speeches on sex. We meet Alcibiades, the incredibly brilliant and good-looking politician who talked Athens into the disastrous Sicilian Expedition, and Aristophanes, the comic poet. Aristophanes' speech is one of the best speeches in all of Plato. The other speech this good is Callicles' talk in the *Gorgias*. If you have read Nietzsche, you will recognize that he got his moral vision from Callicles. Nietzsche never denied that the way to go forward is to go back to the Greeks.

Xenophon's *Conversations of Socrates* is now available from Penguin, including the *Memoirs of Socrates* (traditionally the *Memorabilia*) and his version of the Socrates' *Apology*, which was quite important for I. F. Stone's interpretation in his best-seller, *The Trial of Socrates*. Aristophanes' *Clouds* is a play about Socrates as he seemed to someone who disapproved of his influence on young people. It is often discounted for that reason, wrongly in my opinion. Apart from that problem, it is a great work of literature, as great a comedy as the *Oresteia* and *Antigone* are tragedies. There is no other Greek drama, not even the *Bacchae*, which deals so clearly with our present discontents.

I have not yet mentioned Plato's *Republic* and the great Simile of the Cave which begins Book VII. According to Socrates, the Athenians of his day resemble men sitting in a dark cave, staring at a wall onto which other men, by holding up images in front of a fire, project shadows. The people sitting in the cave think that the reflections on the wall are reality. But one day a man gets up from his seat and turns around. He sees that the reflections are the creations of the people holding up the images. He goes outside and sees the real world and the sun, the source both of life and of knowledge. That is what Plato thought his contemporaries were like. And this is what we have become. We sit in a dark room, watching screens on which play reflections of images manipulated by people we do not see, and we take those reflections for reality. I remember as a teenager, when the local Woolworth's Five and Dime caught on fire. A large crowd gathered to watch. Then about 11:00 p.m. the crowd disappeared. I found out later that they had gone home to watch the fire on television. That, not their own experience, was reality for them. I was surprised. (Frankly I was shocked.) Plato would not have been.

Remember, for the most part you can find the books you need in public libraries, in paperback editions in ordinary bookstores, and in used bookstores. Acquiring Greek and Latin does not cost a lot of money, but it does involve getting up from your seat in the cave and walking out into the sun. As Plato told us, that decision will involve effort and even some pain, because at first the intellectual sunlight is too bright for our minds. So do not expect encouragement from other people in the cave. Getting into the sun does not bring you money or position in life. It does bring you a quality of life you can't find elsewhere; a different type of life, a higher kind of life, under that bright and warm sun that sends its rays streaming to us from the Mediterranean.

INDEX